Parenting Children With Oppositional Defiant Disorder

A Life-Changing Guide to Help Your Defiant Child Overcome ODD Behaviors, Regulate Their Emotions and Stop Backtalk

Erika Bishop

© Copyright 2023 – Erika Bishop – All rights reserved

The content within this book may not be reproduced, duplicated, or transmitted without direct written permission from the author or publisher.

Under no circumstances will any blame or legal responsibility be held against the publisher, or author, for any damages, reparation, or monetary loss due to the information contained within this book, either directly or indirectly.

Legal Notice

This book is copyright protected. This book is only for personal use. You cannot amend, distribute, sell, use, quote, or paraphrase any part, or the content within this book, without the consent of the author or publisher.

Disclaimer Notice

Please note that the information contained within this document is for educational and entertainment purposes only. All effort has been executed to present accurate, up-to-date, and reliable, complete information. No warranties of any kind are declared or implied. Readers acknowledge that the author is not engaging in rendering legal, financial, medical, or professional advice.

Table of Contents

Introduction 5

Part 1: Understanding Oppositional Defiant Disorder 10

Chapter 1: How Are Behaviors Formed? 11

Chapter 2: What is Oppositional Defiant Disorder 18

Chapter 3: Why Is My Child so Angry and Defiant? 24

Chapter 4: Defining Family Roles and Parental Authority 29

Chapter 5: How to Control Your Emotions 35

Chapter 6: Your Child's Behavior Is Not Because of You 39

Part 2: Discipline Strategies for ODD 45

Chapter 7: Basics Skills to Teach Children 46

Chapter 8: Why You Should Avoid Negotiating With Your Children ... 54

Chapter 9: How to Get a Defiant Child to Obey 59

Chapter 10: How to Discipline a Teenager That Will Not Listen 63

Chapter 11: How to Deal With Teenage Temper Tantrums 68

Chapter 12: How to Teach a Child Respect and Discipline 73

Chapter 13: How to Get Kids to Go to Bed 78

Chapter 14: How to Stop Your Kid From Talking Back 85

Chapter 15: How to Punish a Child for Bad Behavior 91

Chapter 16: How to Teach a Kid Not to Hit 94

Chapter 17: Discipline a Teenager Who Does Not Care About Consequences 98

Chapter 18: Parenting Tips 102

Chapter 19: 25 Privileges Children Can Earn for Following the Rules and Having "Good Behavior" 106

Chapter 20: Discipline Tips for Kids With Oppositional Defiant Disorder 110

Part 3: Building Positive Relationships and Communication 114

Chapter 21: Stop Yelling at Your Kids 115

Chapter 22: Best Exercises and Activities for Oppositional Defiant Disorder 119

Chapter 23: The Importance of Building Self-Esteem 124

Chapter 24: Self-Esteem Journal 128

Chapter 25: Get More Cooperation 133

Lend Your Voice to ODD Parenting Support 137

Conclusion 138

About the Author 140

Introduction

Recently, there has been a clear rise in challenging issues, attitudes, and behaviors among children. Parents, teachers, and people who work with kids to help them grow and learn are worried about this trend. Children today often have hard-to-handle traits like defiance, aggression, hyperactivity, and trouble focusing. These problems can hurt a child's schoolwork and social life and be hard for parents and teachers. Not only is it a big problem, but it is also probably the most common thing parents talk about with pediatricians and family doctors, and it is the biggest problem teachers worry about. Teachers often quit because they become overwhelmed with managing the classroom and cannot teach the curriculum properly.

Moreover, it is the number one reason people are sent to mental health services. It is a big, big issue, and I feel like I have learned a lot from these kids, their families, their caretakers, and those who have helped them over the past few years.

When a child acts up, it is important to remember that it is not because they want to act up or cause trouble. As parents or caregivers, we must remember that children do well if they can. Something is stopping a child from doing well if they are not. We should not blame the child for their behavior. Instead, we should figure out what might be holding them back. As people who help the child, we must find ways to help them overcome these problems and encourage good behavior. When we go to a professional for help, like a child development expert or a psychologist, we must be patient and understanding. By thinking this way, we can help our kids better control their feelings and actions, which will help them grow up healthier and make life at home more enjoyable.

Conventional methods of discipline try to get kids to behave better by making them think they do not want to. But you cannot always count on this being true. Recent research shows that kids do well if they can, and if they do not, it is likely because something is getting in their way. As parents or caretakers, we must find out what is stopping them and help them get past it. Punishments and rewards may not be enough to get a child to behave better. Instead, we need to be patient and understanding and get professional help to aid our kids to act well and grow healthy. By taking this approach, we can give our kids a more supportive and caring environment to grow up in.

It is time to admit that what people usually think about kids and how they act is wrong. Neuroscience research has shown that kids who have trouble with their behavior may not be deliberately disobedient or rude. Instead, they may not have the cognitive, emotional, or social skills they need to control their behavior healthily. For kids to behave well, they need to know how to solve problems, be flexible, and deal with frustration, just like they need to know how to read and do mathematics to perform well in school. We need to treat children's difficult behavior with the same understanding and compassion we show to kids with learning disabilities. Previously, kids who had trouble reading were often wrongly called lazy or stupid. It is important to remember that kids who act out may also be misunderstood. We must keep in mind that these kids are working hard, and adults are responsible for helping children acquire the skills they need to succeed.

Let me give you some important thoughts. Even though they always act well and follow the rules, the so-called "good kids" do not always deserve all the praise they get. They do not have to try very hard to act the way they do because it comes naturally to them. On the other hand, kids who act up often have difficulty keeping themselves in check. They may have learning disabilities that affect their ability to solve problems, be flexible, and deal with frustration, which makes it hard to control their behavior.

A wise man once told me that if you call someone something, they will eventually act that way. So, if we treat kids like they are lazy and do not care, they will act that way. Instead, we must acknowledge that kids do well because they are capable, not because they want to. I am sure that all kids want to do well, but some have delays in their development that make it hard for them to do so. For example, two-year-olds often act badly because they do not have the skills they need, like being flexible, solving problems, and dealing with frustration. But as they grow up, many learn these skills and act better. Some kids, though, may be behind in certain areas of development.

When adults stop blaming kids for their actions and try to understand what is going on in their lives and find ways to help them, amazing things can happen. Instead of telling a child to try harder to behave, it is important to figure out what is causing their bad behavior and give them the help they need.

This can happen when a child has problems with their behavior because the child's brain is still developing, and parts of the brain that help with self-control and emotional regulation are not fully grown yet. It cannot be fixed by putting the child in a different learning program or getting a tutor. Instead, it may require specific interventions that target those areas of development, such as teaching them certain ways to deal with their emotions or improving their social skills. Children can learn these skills and act better if they get the right help. Predictable problems like getting ready for school, deciding what to wear and eat, setting limits on screen time, and doing homework can help kids practice these skills. Changing adults' thinking from "Kids can do well" to "Kids do well if they can," enables them to work with kids to solve problems and help them develop these skills. This process involves using empathy to figure out what a child is worried about, sharing worries but not solutions, and asking the child to help come up with solutions that work for both of you. This simple method can be used with kids of all ages and for big and small problems. When used in homes, schools, treatment centers, jails, and even by the police, the results are amazing.

As parents, it is important to work with our kids to solve common problems around the house, like the morning routine. This means taking care of a problem that is likely to happen with empathy and understanding. Once we know what our child is worried about, we can talk to them about it so that everyone gets out the door on time and has a good start to the day. At this point, it is important not to jump in with our ideas for fixing the problem. Instead, we should let our children come up with ideas. By working together in this way, we can develop solutions that work for everyone and make the house a better place to live in. So, let us look at your child's problems with understanding, compassion, and a willingness to work together.

Collaborative problem-solving can help kids who have trouble solving problems, being flexible, and dealing with frustration. It can also help adults in places like the workplace and partnerships. Some kids are born with these skills, but it is important to help the kids practice them through this process. This helps them prepare for future challenges and learn useful skills for the 21st century. By working together to solve problems, we can reduce difficult behavior, improve relationships, and help kids and adults solve problems better and be flexible. Let us empower our children with the skills they need to succeed.

Kids who are hard to teach should get the same kind, caring, and effective help as kids with other learning disabilities. Why? Because I think all kids want to do well, and if they are not, it is not just because they do not want to. Most of the time, it is because they do not have the right skills. But if you have the skills, you will find a way. So, let us work together to teach your child how to resolve conflicts, be adaptable, and handle frustration.

The strategies and techniques provided in this book are aimed at helping children learn how to effectively manage and overcome challenging situations, including dealing with feelings of frustration.

By implementing these strategies, parents can help their children develop the necessary skills to succeed in various aspects of their lives, including their academic, personal, and professional pursuits. Parents can build better relationships with their children, reduce challenging behavior, and create a more positive and peaceful home environment using these approaches. The main focus is on how important it is to practice these skills with children and adults to improve our ability to solve problems in a way that is good for everyone. This book offers valuable insights and tools for parents to help their children thrive and succced.

Part 1:
Understanding Oppositional Defiant Disorder

Chapter 1:
How Are Behaviors Formed?

Human behavior refers to the physical, mental, and social activities throughout a person's life. These activities follow a typical pattern of growth that can be divided into distinct stages, including prenatal life, infancy, childhood, adolescence, and adulthood. While human development is a lifelong process, most scientific research has focused on the first 12 years of life due to the significant and rapid psychological changes that occur during this period and their role in shaping mental functioning in adulthood.

Theories of Development

The study of children and their development is a relatively new field, with most research done since the 1940s. For a long time, psychologists argued whether genetic or environmental factors were more important in determining a child's growth. However, it is now recognized that both play a role. Cognitive abilities, emotions, and behavior are influenced by biological factors (like genetics) and external factors (like experiences and social environment).

In the 20th century, three prominent theories of human development emerged, each addressing different aspects of psychological development. However, these and other theories have limitations and do not fully explain all aspects of development. Therefore, most research in the field is descriptive, and there is no single framework that can provide complete explanations for all aspects of development.

1. Psychoanalytic Theories

Sigmund Freud, an Austrian neurologist who developed psychoanalytic theories, is also known as the father of psychoanalysis.

His ideas were influenced by Charles Darwin's theory of evolution and the concept of energy applied to the central nervous system.

According to Freud, a person's inborn, inherited drives and instinctual forces are contained in an unconscious mental structure called the id. The ego, the reality-oriented portion of the personality, develops during infancy and childhood to balance and complement the id. The ego uses conscious and unconscious mental processes to satisfy id instincts while also trying to maintain the individual comfortably in relation to the environment.

Freud believed that child development primarily concerns the emergence of the ego's functions. The ego controls intellectual and perceptual functions while channeling the discharge of virtual drives and negotiating realistically with the outside world. Erik Erikson, a German-born American psychoanalyst, modified Freud's ideas to include psychosocial and social factors in personality development.

Erikson established eight stages of emotional development over the life span, each with important inner conflicts that must be successfully resolved to avoid personality problems. The first four stages are:

- Infancy: trust versus mistrust
- Early childhood: autonomy versus shame/doubt
- Preschool: initiative versus guilt
- School age: industry versus inferiority

2. Piaget's Theory

Jean Piaget was a psychologist who wanted to understand how adults learn to think logically and make sense of the world. He believed that children go through four stages of cognitive development as they grow up, each building on the previous one. In the first stage, from birth to 2 years, children learn by interacting with objects around them. For example, they may learn that a tower of blocks can be knocked down and rebuilt. As they move through the stages, their thinking becomes more sophisticated, and they learn new concepts, such as reversibility, which helps them solve problems more effectively. Finally, in the last stage, which characterizes adolescence and adulthood, people can think rationally and systematically about hypothetical problems, even if they do not have direct experience with them. Piaget's theory helps us understand how children learn and develop their thinking abilities.

3. Learning Theory

Learning theory is a way of understanding how children learn and develop their behaviors and values. It emphasizes the effects of reward and punishment on the child's actions rather than on their emotions or thoughts. There are two types of learning processes; classical and instrumental conditioning. Classical conditioning creates an association between two stimuli, while instrumental conditioning creates a relationship between a response and a stimulus. Rewards, like praise and approval, encourage children to repeat certain behaviors, while punishments discourage them. Scientists use these principles to explain how children's behavior changes as they grow and develop.

Many factors can play a role in child misbehavior. It is crucial to understand these causes for effective behavior management and correction. Several psychological theories can explain children's misbehavior.

- **Attachment Theory**

    This theory is a psychological one that John Bowlby developed in the 1950s. It suggests that the relationship between a child and their primary caregiver (usually the mother) in the first few years of life significantly impacts the child's emotional and social development. Bowlby argued that infants are biologically programmed to seek out close and affectionate relationships with their caregivers. These early attachment experiences influence the child's internal working model of relationships and can shape their behavior and emotional regulation in later life. The theory also suggests that attachment is a two-way street, with caregivers forming emotional bonds with their children that influence their behavior and parenting style.

- **Behavioral Theory**

    Behavioral theory proposes that behavior is learned through experience and shaped by the consequences that follow it. The theory suggests that behavior reinforced with rewards is more likely to be repeated, while behavior that is punished is less likely to be repeated. Behaviorists focus on observable behaviors and use conditioning techniques, such as operant conditioning, to modify behavior. Behavioral theory is often used in therapy to help people overcome maladaptive behaviors or phobias.

- **Cognitive-Behavioral Theory**

    The cognitive-behavioral theory (CBT) is a psychological approach that combines elements of the cognitive theory (which emphasizes the role of thoughts and beliefs in shaping behavior) with the behavioral theory. The theory suggests that people's behavior is influenced by their thoughts, feelings, and beliefs about themselves, others, and the world around them. These thoughts, feelings, and beliefs can be either helpful or unhelpful, leading to positive or negative outcomes. CBT aims to help people identify and change negative thinking and behavior patterns.

- **Social Learning Theory**

    Observation and imitation are key components of social learning theory. This theory was developed by Albert Bandura in the 1960s and 1970s and is based on the idea that people are active agents in their learning. The social learning theory emphasizes the importance of modeling and reinforcement in shaping behavior. It suggests that people are likelier to imitate rewarded or reinforced behaviors and less likely to imitate punished or ignored behaviors. This theory has been applied in several fields, including education, parenting, and health promotion.

Parenting Styles

Human development is a complex process that is influenced by a combination of genetics, biology, culture, and experiences. Development in one area of life can affect development in others, and these influences interact over time. But there is one factor that no one can overlook. Parenting is about shaping our children's behavior, one of our most important responsibilities. Many factors influence our children's behavior and development, but parenting style and practice play a crucial role. Different parenting styles and practices impact children's behavior differently.

Parents can be authoritarian, authoritative, permissive, or uninvolved.

- Authoritarian parents are strict, demanding, and controlling. They expect obedience from their children, and there is little room for negotiation or compromise. Authoritarian parents may use punishment as a means of discipline.

- Authoritative parents are firm but fair. They set clear boundaries and rules, but they also allow their children to express themselves and provide explanations for their decisions. They use positive reinforcement to encourage good behavior.

- Permissive parents are more relaxed and lenient. They may avoid setting boundaries and rules and focus more on being their child's friend than their parent. They may use few or no consequences for misbehavior.

- Uninvolved parents are hands-off and detached. They may be too busy or preoccupied to provide adequate support and guidance for their children. They may have little interest in their child's life.

Children's behavior is also influenced by how parents interact with them daily. The most important parenting practices include positive reinforcement, discipline, communication, and modeling behavior. Positive reinforcement involves praising and rewarding good behavior. This can be anything from verbal acknowledgment to a special treat or outing. Discipline helps children learn right from wrong and make better choices. Consistent consequences for misbehavior, such as time-outs or loss of privileges, can be effective. Communication is key to building a strong relationship with your child. Listening to your child's thoughts and feelings and providing guidance is essential for their emotional development. Modeling behavior is also essential. Parents who model healthy and positive behaviors are likelier to have children who follow suit.

Parenting styles and practices can significantly impact children's emotional development, social skills, academic performance, and risky behaviors. Children with authoritative parents tend to have better emotional development and social skills, while those with uninvolved parents may struggle. Children with authoritarian parents may do well academically but struggle with self-esteem and independence. Children with permissive parents may struggle with impulse control and may engage in more risky behaviors.

Understanding the Root Causes of Child Misbehavior

As parents and caregivers, dealing with child misbehavior can be challenging. While some may attribute it to bad behavior, it is important to understand the contributing factors and psychological theories behind it.

Child temperament and personality traits play a significant role in their behavior. Some children may be naturally more impulsive or stubborn, making them more prone to misbehavior. Family and environmental factors, such as parenting styles and peer influence, can also majorly impact children's behavior. Another contributing factor is developmentally inappropriate expectations. Children may act out when pushed beyond their abilities or subjected to unrealistic expectations. Adapting expectations to the child's developmental stage is important. One common reason for misbehavior is a lack of social and emotional skills. Children who struggle with communication or emotion regulation may act out to express themselves or get attention.

Understanding these contributing factors and psychological theories can help parents and caregivers better manage child misbehavior. By addressing the root causes and employing effective strategies, such as positive reinforcement and communication skills, parents can help children develop more positive behaviors and improve their social and emotional skills. By adopting a positive parenting style and implementing effective parenting practices, parents can help their children develop into happy, healthy, and successful adults. Being a responsible parent and spending time and energy building a strong relationship with your child is important. The benefits will last a lifetime.

Remember, it takes patience, consistency, and a willingness to work with each child's unique temperament and needs.

Chapter 2:
What is Oppositional Defiant Disorder

A continuous pattern of rebellion and hostility toward adults in authority characterizes oppositional defiant disorder (ODD). This disorder is a relatively common behavioral disorder typically developing in childhood or adolescence. This chapter will discuss the symptoms, causes, diagnosis, and approach toward ODD.

Definition of Oppositional Defiant Disorder

Oppositional defiant disorder is a behavioral disorder that affects children and adolescents. According to the DSM-5 (Diagnostic and Statistical Manual of Mental Disorders, Fifth Edition), ODD is characterized by negative, defiant, disobedient, and hostile behavior toward authority figures that persists for at least six months.

Prevalence of Oppositional Defiant Disorder

Oppositional defiant disorder is one of the most conventional behavioral disorders in children and adolescents. According to the DSM-5, the occurrence of ODD in the general population is around 1-11%. The prevalence is higher in children with attention deficit hyperactivity disorder (ADHD) or other behavioral disorders.

Symptoms of Oppositional Defiant Disorder

Children often first show signs of oppositional defiant disorder in early elementary school. Even though ODD can sometimes manifest later in life, it often starts before adolescence. There is a persistent pattern of behavior that is both hostile and defiant.

Children and adolescents with ODD often exhibit defiant behavior toward authority figures such as parents, teachers, and other adults.

They may argue with adults, refuse to comply with rules, and deliberately annoy others.

- Anger and irritability: ODD can cause children and adolescents to be easily angered, irritable, and have frequent temper outbursts. They may have difficulty managing their emotions, leading to aggressive behavior.

- Vindictiveness and spitefulness: Children with ODD may be vindictive and spiteful toward others. They may seek revenge or hold grudges against others they perceive have wronged them.

- Non-compliance and rebellion: Children with ODD frequently refuse to follow the rules and instructions. They may deliberately break the rules or engage in behavior that authority figures prohibit.

- Negative attitude and stubbornness: Children and adolescents with ODD often have a negative attitude toward authority figures and may be stubborn and resistant to change. They may have difficulty accepting criticism or feedback from others.

A negative, disobedient, and aggressive behavior pattern can make it hard for the child to do well in school, with friends, and later at work. An example of ODD behavior is a child who always fights with their parents and refuses to do what they tell them to do. For instance, the child may refuse to go to bed at the time set by their parents, even after being repeatedly reminded. When their parents try to make them follow the rules, they may yell, throw fits, or get violent.

The child may also have a pattern of not following rules and acting out at school. They might not want to follow the rules, argue with their teachers, and make learning hard for their classmates. This behavior could cause problems in school, like getting behind on work or not finishing assignments.

In social situations, a child with ODD may be mean to other kids and adults, which makes it hard for them to make and keep friends. They may have a bad attitude and be stubborn around people in charge, which can cause problems and tension in relationships. Overall, ODD can show up differently, but it is defined by a pattern of persistent defiance and hostility toward authority figures, making it hard for the child to do things.

Causes of Oppositional Defiant Disorder

1. Genetics

Research suggests that genetics play a role in the development of oppositional defiant disorder. Studies have shown that children with ODD are more likely to have family members with behavioral disorders, including attention deficit hyperactivity disorder (ADHD), conduct disorder, and substance abuse disorder.

2. Environmental Factors

Environmental factors, including exposure to trauma or abuse, poverty, and parental conflict, can increase the risk of developing oppositional defiant disorder. Children who experience adverse childhood events are more likely to develop behavioral disorders, including ODD.

3. Parenting Style

Parenting style can also play a role in the development of oppositional defiant disorder. Parents who are inconsistent in their discipline or use harsh punishment may increase the risk of their child developing ODD.

4. Social and Cultural Influences

Peer pressure and other social and cultural factors can also cause the development of oppositional defiant disorder. Children with friends who engage in defiant or aggressive behavior may be more likely to exhibit similar behavior.

5. **Neurological Factors**

Research suggests that neurological factors, including abnormalities in brain structure and function, may contribute to the development of oppositional defiant disorder. Studies have shown that children with ODD have different brain activity and structure than children without the disorder.

It can be complicated to figure out what causes ODD in a child because it is usually a mix of genetic, environmental, social, and neurological causes. Seeking help from a mental health professional specializing in child behavior disorders and considering the child's family history, environment, and parenting style can help determine what might be causing ODD and create a treatment plan that fits the child's needs.

Diagnosis and Treatment of Oppositional Defiant Disorder

The diagnosis of oppositional defiant disorder involves a thorough assessment of the child's behavior and symptoms. The DSM-5 provides precise diagnostic criteria for ODD; your healthcare provider can guide you well. Assessment tools for ODD may include parent and teacher interviews, behavioral rating scales, and direct observation of the child's behavior. It is important to assess for other co-occurring disorders, such as attention deficit hyperactivity disorder (ADHD), anxiety, and depression, as they may impact the course and treatment of ODD.

Treatment for ODD typically involves a multimodal approach, including behavioral and family therapy, medication, and school-based interventions.

- Behavioral therapy focuses on teaching the child coping skills and strategies for managing their behavior. Therapy aims to improve the child's social and emotional functioning and reduce disruptive behavior.

- Family therapy involves working with the child's parents or caregivers to improve parenting skills and communication within the family. Family therapy can also help reduce conflict and improve relationships between family members.

- Medication may be used in some cases to treat symptoms of oppositional defiant disorder, such as aggression and irritability. Medications commonly used for ODD include stimulants, antidepressants, and antipsychotics.

- School-based interventions may also help address ODD. This may include accommodations and modifications to the child's academic and social environment and using positive reinforcement and behavior management strategies.

Importance of Early Intervention

When it comes to treating an oppositional defiant disorder, early intervention is crucial. Children with ODD who receive early intervention are more likely to have positive outcomes, including improved social and academic functioning and reduced disruptive behavior. Early intervention may also reduce the risk of developing more severe behavioral disorders like conduct disorders. With appropriate treatment, children with the disorder can experience significant improvement in their behavior and functioning. Behavioral therapy and family therapy are effective in reducing the symptoms of ODD and improving family relationships.

Research on ODD is ongoing, focusing on improving our understanding of the disorder's causes and mechanisms. Future research may also focus on developing new and more effective treatments for ODD and identifying ways to prevent the development of the disorder. Overall, continued research on ODD is critical in improving our ability to diagnose, treat, and prevent this common behavioral disorder.

It can be difficult and stressful to parent a child with ODD, and you may often feel helpless and alone. Despite this, you must always remember that you are not alone in this and that you can get better together as a family. This book looks at the disorder from a new angle and suggests a new way to help kids with ODD. It is a useful resource to help you learn more about the disorder and give you tools and strategies for dealing with your child's behavior. Getting closer to your child and helping them deal with the problems that come with ODD is possible if you get the right help and support.

Chapter 3:
Why Is My Child so Angry and Defiant?

As parents, it can be frustrating and confusing when our children become defiant and act out in anger. We may wonder what we did wrong or why our child behaves this way. It is important to understand that there are many reasons why children become defiant, and it is not always because they are simply being difficult. By taking the time to understand the root causes of our children's behavior, we can help them overcome their defiance and build stronger relationships with them. In this chapter, we will explore some common reasons why children become defiant and how we can support them through these challenges.

Although no one enjoys feeling angry, it is a common emotion experienced by individuals of all ages. However, many adults struggle to express anger in healthy and productive ways, resulting in outbursts for children. Parents may wonder how to handle their child's angry behavior and whether it is typical or problematic. When should parents be worried about their child's anger, irritability, and aggression? While it is not unusual for children under the age of four to have up to nine tantrums per week, featuring crying, kicking, stomping, hitting, and pushing that last for five to ten minutes, most children grow out of this behavior by kindergarten. If a child's tantrums persist and become developmentally inappropriate, seeking professional assistance may be necessary.

Multiple factors may contribute to a child's anger, irritability, and aggression difficulties. Anger issues are frequently linked with other mental health issues in children, including attention deficit hyperactivity disorder (ADHD), autism, obsessive-compulsive disorder (OCD), and Tourette's syndrome. Anger and aggression may be influenced by genetics and other biological factors, as well as the environment. Trauma, family dysfunction, and particular parenting approaches, such as harsh and inconsistent punishment, may all contribute to a child's likelihood of exhibiting anger and aggression that interferes with their daily life.

We live in a time when some people might say that defiant children are the norm and that anger is just a normal part of most people's lives. This has not always been the case, and it does not have to be. But then what is it about our kids that makes them so stubborn and angry?

Through this book, I want to help you understand how some of your kids might feel about it. A child may display defiance or aggression for various reasons, and what is going on in their mind depends on the individual child's unique circumstances and experiences. Below are some common factors that can contribute to a child's defiant or aggressive behavior:

- Children have limited control over their environment and often desire things out of their reach. When a child cannot obtain what they want or are required to do something they do not feel like doing, they may feel frustrated. This frustration may arise from feeling powerless or lacking control over their situation. For example, a child may want a particular toy, but their parent or caregiver may not be able to purchase it for them. Alternatively, they may be required to eat a particular food that they do not enjoy, or they may be required to perform a task that they find difficult. When faced with these situations, children may feel a range of emotions, including disappointment, sadness, and anger. If a child does not have the tools to manage these emotions, they may respond with defiance or aggression. For instance, a child frustrated because they cannot have a toy may throw a tantrum or become aggressive toward others. Similarly, a child who is required to eat a particular food they do not enjoy may refuse to eat or become aggressive toward their parent or caregiver.

- Younger children are still developing their capacity for self-reliance. Aggression may emerge from a place of frustration and helplessness over their situation. They may act aggressively to assert dominance over others or rebel against their parents' attempts to establish a routine. They may gain a false sense of mastery over their surroundings and the actions of others by partaking in such conduct. However, this is counterproductive and can lead to undesirable outcomes like social isolation or punishment. Understanding that children's aggression may stem from a need for independence and control is crucial. We can help children learn more effective coping skills and rely less on aggressive behavior if we give them age-appropriate opportunities for independence and control and teach them healthy ways to express their emotions.

- Children have a natural need for attention and recognition from their caregivers. When they feel neglected or unnoticed, they may act out to get attention, even if that means engaging in negative behaviors. Children may not fully understand the difference between positive and negative attention; negative attention can be better than no attention. This can lead to negative behaviors that continue until the child receives the attention they crave. Parents or caregivers can unintentionally reinforce this behavior by giving more attention to negative behaviors than positive ones. For example, if a child is acting out and the parent responds with yelling or punishment, the child may learn that acting out is a surefire way to get attention from their caregiver. Therefore, it is important to focus on reinforcing positive behaviors and ignoring minor negative behaviors that are not dangerous or harmful.

- Emotional dysregulation is a child's inability to regulate or control their emotions. This can make it challenging for them to handle their feelings appropriately. When children feel overwhelmed, stressed, or upset, they may react with defiance or aggression. They may feel like they have no control over their emotions and lash out to release their feelings.

- One more reason anger and defiance are rising is that they are in style. Did you know many kids feel weak if they are not angry and defiant these days? They keep doing it because they think that is how strong people act. It would help if they were rude, angry, and bold instead of crying, worrying, and being scared.

- Anxiety is another reason why so many children get angry. They do feel much fear; fear of failing. Maybe you give them a job to do, but they have never done it before, do not remember how to do it, or are perfectionists who are not sure if they will do it right. They may not attempt to explain their worries or feelings because they know it may be difficult to put them into words. Instead, they may focus on processing their feelings or seeking support from others. They get angry about it because it makes them upset and anxious.

- Sometimes they might become angry or frustrated and say something hurtful or rude. In these situations, they often know that what they said was not an effective or productive way to communicate. They may realize that their words have caused more harm than good and that their message was not received as intended. This can indicate poor communication skills or an inability to manage emotions effectively. Many kids get angry and act out because they want to be noticed.

- Sometimes they are just copying what their parents do. Even though it is hard to hear, sometimes parents tell their kids not to do the same things they do themselves. So, if you have anger and stubbornness, ensure you get the help you need. Find out what makes you calm, and get the tools to stay calm.

- Some kids may choose anger because it gives them a false sense of strength and happiness, like winning a competition. Everyone who watches it knows it is a lie. However, the child doing it is unaware of this, as they are losing. They can always take control of their situation and improve it if they make the right choice.

Children may do bad things to get their caregivers' attention or because they cannot control their emotions. But it is important to remember that anger and defiance are not always bad and can be fixed with the right management techniques. In the upcoming chapters, we will discuss how to deal with and control these behaviors in children. Using the right methods, we can help kids learn how to control their feelings and actions, which is good for the child and their caretakers.

Chapter 4:
The Importance of Defining Family Roles and Parental Authority

Establishing clear responsibilities within the family is crucial to maintaining positive communication and cooperation. It entails figuring out what roles each person plays in the family and what is expected of them. Clarifying expectations, reducing arguments, and boosting communication are all facilitated by establishing clear roles within the family. In this chapter, we will discuss why it is important to identify roles in the family, what the different roles are, and how to define them.

Family members benefit greatly when clear boundaries and expectations are recognized by establishing clearly defined roles. Everyone benefits when every person in the household understands their place and knows what to anticipate from one another. As a result, there may be less room for argument and more room for collaboration.

Roles Within a Family

Family roles can change depending on family size, composition, cultural norms, and societal expectations. Nonetheless, some typical duties in a family are:

- Caregiver: First and foremost, the caregiver must take care of a loved one in need, whether a youngster, an aging relative, or someone with special needs.

- Provider: The provider is responsible for bringing in money for the household, either through regular employment or self-employment.

- Mediator: A mediator may be called to mediate disagreements and confrontations amongst family members, such as between siblings or parents and children.
- Disciplinarian: The disciplinarian is responsible for maintaining norms and limits within the family, such as establishing consequences for bad behavior and enforcing curfews for teenagers.

The Challenge of Establishing Clear Boundaries Within the Family

Although it may be difficult, defining duties within the family is essential to its well-being. These are some guidelines for establishing clear family dynamics:

- Determine What Your Family Requires: Seeing that every family is distinct and every member has specific requirements, it is important to determine what your family requires. That is why assessing the household's requirements is crucial before settling on job descriptions. Think about the needs of everyone in the family, the jobs that must be done, and the unique skills each family member may offer.
- Define the Roles and Duties: After establishing what your family needs, you can start thinking about how to get it. Cooking, cleaning, taking care of children, and managing money are just a few examples of responsibilities that may be broken down into smaller, more manageable tasks.
- Designate Functions: After determining what needs to be done, the following step is to divide up the work among the household members. Assign work based on each team member's strengths and interests. It is also crucial to divide up work fairly among team members.

- Explain Your Part: Once responsibilities have been divided, they must be made known to everyone in the household. Please specify what you anticipate from each individual in their assigned function. Listen to everyone in the family, including their suggestions and complaints, and work together to find solutions.
- Rethinking Your Acts: It is important to go back and reevaluate responsibilities every so often to ensure they still reflect the current state of the family. Check to see if everyone is pulling their weight, and if not, discuss potential adjustments as a unit.

Parental Authority

The term "parental authority" describes a parent's legal right to make choices on behalf of and enforce rules upon their kid. This power is grounded in the idea that parents know best for their children and should be free to make choices allowing them to flourish and develop in a secure and loving setting. All parents have to protect their children legally and morally from harm.

The ability to influence one's children is crucial for effective parenting. This allows parents to make choices on their children's behalf and establish limits and standards for their conduct. Adherence to and respect for parental authority is a cornerstone of happy family life, and they flourish when children learn to accept and embrace their role as subordinates.

A parent's job entails more than merely enforcing rules and threatening consequences. Parents should give their children a predictable, secure, and nurturing environment to develop. Identify your family's core values and establish norms that will assist in upholding them. Have a family meeting and go over the house rules with your kids. There are a variety of resources you can turn to for guidance if you find yourself stuck. There will likely be a parenting resource center near you, whether you live in a small town or a large city. You might enroll in a class on nurturing parenting to gain insight into how to best interact with your children and what principles to instill in your household.

Parental power includes but is not limited to establishing and enforcing rules and expectations for behavior, making the child's education and health-related decisions, and administering appropriate punishments for misbehavior. The proper exercise of parental authority aids in setting limits and expectations for children, encouraging them to act responsibly.

A Guide to Establishing and Maintaining Your Authority as a Parent

The parental authority must be established and upheld, despite possible difficulties. Here are some suggestions for establishing and sustaining one's parental authority:

- Maintaining your authority as a parent requires that you be consistent with your discipline and expectations. Kids must understand what is expected of them and what will happen if they do not comply with the rules. Ensure both parents are on the same page regarding rules and punishments and consistently apply these.

- Establishing one's authority as a parent requires open and honest communication. Explain the repercussions of breaking the rules and expectations you have set. Let your child express their worries and questions, and be ready to defend your parenting choices.

- In front of their children, parents should model responsible behavior. Be the example of the person you want your child to become by acting responsibly.

- It is necessary to enforce rules and consequences with firmness, but it is also crucial to do so in a caring and supporting manner. Even when you must reprimand your child, show them you care about them and want the best for them.

Let me give you an example. Each day after school, a parent expects their child to sit down and finish their assignment. The parent clarifies that homework comes before any free time or screen time. In addition, parents make it clear that they expect their kids to reach out for assistance when they get stuck on their assignments. The parent establishes authority and advises the youngster by laying down this rule and expectation. The kid knows what is required of them and realizes the importance of finishing their schoolwork. The child and parent can benefit from a more streamlined and productive approach to homework time. More importantly, the kid is learning to comply with adult directives, which can set the stage for future academic and professional success.

The Positive Effects of Establishing Clear Parental Control and Family Roles

- **Better Understanding**

    When everyone knows their place and the parents are respected, everyone in the household can speak more openly with one another. Communication at home must be kept open and peaceful by establishing ground rules and clear expectations for everyone.

- **Decreased Conflicts Among Family Members**

    Having defined responsibilities and authorities in the home might lessen friction among family members. Disagreements and miscommunications are less likely to arise when everyone is clear on their responsibilities.

- **Improved Family Unity**

    Promoting family unity is facilitated by clearly defining parental authority and family duties. The bonds of a family are strengthened when each member understands their place and contributes to the achievement of shared goals.

- **Improved Capacity for Making Choices**

    Parents need to feel confident in their authority to make the best choices for their kids. Therefore, any decision that must be made will always be based on the child's welfare and the development of stable relationships within families.

Healthy family dynamics can be established through clear roles and parental authority. Youngsters with a healthy respect for their parents' authority are likelier to feel safe and content.

Establishing parental authority and clearly defining family roles is crucial for a harmonious household. Families can better meet all members' needs and divide work more evenly by establishing clear responsibilities for everyone. Parents may more effectively supervise and teach their children when they have established their authority and follow it consistently. Adopting these habits can result in positive communication, family cohesion, decision-making, and dynamic health changes. Establishing parental control and defining family responsibilities can be difficult, but the long-term advantages are worth the effort. Families can grow and support each other better if these norms are implemented as a unit.

Chapter 5:
How to Control Your Emotions

Do your emotions sometimes trouble you a lot? The main idea of this chapter is to discuss how to control your emotions as a parent.

Maintaining composure as a parent is essential. It is the ability to control and direct one's emotions, especially in trying circumstances. When parents can control their emotions, they are better positioned to make objective choices that put their children's health, safety, and development first. In doing so, parents and children are more likely to develop relationships characterized by mutual trust, admiration, and open dialogue. Children learn best when their parents practice what they preach, and parents who can regulate their emotions set a great example. Emotional regulation helps parents feel less overwhelmed, which allows them to be more present and engaged with their children. A healthy and supportive family atmosphere is fostered when parents exhibit positive parenting skills, including active listening, praise, and empathy.

Our emotions are part of who we are and can be good or bad. They can help us bond with others and feel love and kindness but they can also lead to negative emotions like anger and jealousy. When we feel something, we have a little thought that follows it, and what we do with it makes all the difference. Emotional freedom and emotional intelligence are about choosing to use our emotions in good ways and being in control of our lives. We can let go of emotions and choose not to have them without stuffing them down or hiding them. We can use a five-step skill set to control our emotions by recognizing, stopping, asking ourselves if we are calm, choosing the words we say, and acting deliberately.

1. **Exercise Self-Government**

The ability to understand the cause and effect of a situation and having knowledge of your behaviors to control them is what self-government is all about. If you wish to manage your emotions in real time, it is important to acknowledge that you possess the power to regulate and govern them and learn the necessary steps. Therefore, the initial step is acknowledging that you can indeed exercise self-government.

2. **Analyze**

To gain control over your emotions, examining your inner state is essential. When you experience a certain feeling, it is crucial to identify its origin. Was it triggered by a thought or action? Did a skipped breakfast contribute to it? Did a personal issue with someone cause you to take it personally? Understanding the reason behind your emotional response is essential, and you can change your thoughts to manage them effectively. For example, if you have a negative thought, such as "I cannot believe they said that to me," you can replace it with a more positive one, such as "I wonder what they want me to understand." You can better alter your thoughts and manage your emotions by shifting your mindset from accusatory to understanding. The key is to analyze yourself, understand your emotions and desired outcomes, and examine the thoughts you generate. This way, you can take control, redirect yourself, and regain your focus.

3. **Make a Plan**

To gain control over your emotions, preparing yourself in advance is crucial. When negative thoughts arise, planning how you will handle them at the moment is vital. This includes planning the specific words you will use when speaking to your spouse, children, or anyone else and writing them down if necessary. Additionally, it is important to plan your body language and how you will conduct yourself to maintain a calm demeanor and positive tone. You can even practice in front of a mirror, rehearsing your words and body language.

Also, consider the type of relationship you want with the person you are speaking with. You can disagree with or correct them while maintaining a connection and bond with them. By planning to care about the person and bond with them, you can have a positive experience, even if you disagree. Preparing yourself in advance can help you control your emotions and effectively manage challenging situations.

4. Act Deliberately

To deliberately take action means to do something intentionally. Therefore, after making a plan, you need to act on it when the situation arises. When you experience a triggering thought or emotion, rather than allowing it to control you, use it as a signal to follow the new dialogue you have planned, even if you need to read it. The same trigger that used to push you over the edge can now be the trigger to stop and take action according to your plan. This involves sensing the trigger, stopping yourself, and giving yourself instructions. People often forget to instruct themselves, even though they instruct their children, employees, and pets. Self-government involves regularly instructing yourself to move towards your goals and grow into the person you want to be in your relationships and any situation.

5. Communicate Effectively

Effective communication is not just about how we interact with others but also how we communicate with ourselves. Emotions often act as a catalyst for change, prompting us to go in a new direction. However, once we have deliberately acted on our plan, we must evaluate how we did it. By self-reflecting, we can prepare for similar situations in the future. It is important to be honest with ourselves, acknowledging what we did well and what adjustments we can make next time. We can return to it or make other necessary adjustments if we forget to follow our plan. Effective communication also involves self-correction. Self-governed individuals are not afraid to correct themselves.

Emotional regulation may appear to be an insurmountable challenge. Yet, with enough repetition, it might eventually feel like second nature. A good friend said to me a few years ago, "I have been calm for an entire year, and now I can honestly say I am at peace." This process is not instantaneous. Maybe you need additional mindfulness and self-control abilities to manage your emotions. Get the support you need to learn how to manage your feelings and put them to good use. Your serenity will be the strength you need to make your relationships more meaningful and your endeavors more fruitful.

Chapter 6:
How Do You Explain to People That Your Child's Behavior Is Not Because of You?

Oppositional defiant disorder can have a significant impact on a child's life. Children with this condition may struggle with relationships at home and school. They may have difficulty making friends, and their behavior may lead to disciplinary action or expulsion from school. Children with ODD may also risk developing other mental health disorders, like anxiety or depression; on the other hand, parents of an ODD child also face difficulties and emotional exhaustion. When a child is diagnosed with this disorder, it can be a challenging experience for the child and their family. Unfortunately, there is often a lack of understanding and awareness surrounding ODD, which can lead to humiliation and judgment from others.

The stigma surrounding ODD can significantly impact parents of children with this condition. Children with this disorder often have difficulty following rules, so their behavior can be disruptive and challenging. Parents of children with ODD may face shame and discrimination from others who do not understand the condition. People may wrongly assume that a child's behavior results from poor parenting or a lack of discipline. This disgrace can harm parents struggling to manage their child's behavior. Parents may feel guilty, ashamed, or embarrassed about their child's behavior, even though they are not responsible. They become more isolated and lonelier.

The sources of judgment and misunderstanding can come from various places, including family members, friends, educators, and even strangers. Family members may struggle to understand why a child behaves a certain way, leading to frustration and blame. Friends and educators may not be aware of the child's diagnosis, leading to confusion and negative reactions. Strangers may publicly witness a child's outburst and make assumptions about the child's behavior and parenting. The potential source of judgment and misunderstanding around ODD is the belief that it is solely caused by bad parenting or a lack of discipline. However, this disorder is a complex condition with various possible causes, including genetics, brain chemistry, and environmental factors. Children with ODD may struggle with defiance, aggression, and irritability, which can be challenging for others. This can lead to negative reactions from other parents or teachers who may not understand the underlying cause of these behaviors.

What Should Parents With an Oppositional Defiant Disorder Child Do?

One of the very first steps is acknowledging that this disorder exists. Many people have misconceptions about ODD, assuming it results from bad parenting or simply a phase that will pass. It is important to understand that this disorder is a real and complex mental health condition that requires support and treatment. By acknowledging this, parents can better prepare themselves for potential negative reactions from others and develop strategies to address them. Those who have not experienced parenting a child with ODD will be unable to comprehend the challenges that come with it. It is crucial to trust one's instincts when raising a child, even if it is difficult to ignore the opinions of others. Letting others' viewpoints influence one's parenting decisions is not advisable.

Parents must develop coping strategies for negative reactions and ODD's stigma. The following may be included:

- Finding support groups or online forums where they can connect with other parents who have similar experiences.

- Seeking a mental health professional or therapist can also be beneficial in developing coping strategies and providing emotional support.
- Parents can also consider speaking out publicly about their experiences with ODD to help raise awareness and reduce the stigma surrounding the condition.

Parents can deal with negative reactions using various tactics, including simple explanations and in-depth discussions. For example, if a stranger witnesses a child's outburst in public, a simple explanation that the child has a behavioral disorder can go a long way in preventing negative assumptions. If a family member struggles to understand ODD, a conversation about the disorder and how it affects the child can help dispel misconceptions and foster understanding.

Or if, despite all your efforts, someone is not ready to understand your point of view, use the gray rock technique. To use this technique to shut someone up, you can try the following:

- Keep your responses brief and straightforward: When someone says something you disagree with or find confrontational, respond with a simple and unemotional statement. Avoid getting defensive or engaging in an argument.
- Avoid sharing personal information or opinions: The goal is to be as uninteresting as possible, so avoid sharing any information that the person might find engaging or could lead to a discussion.
- Do not react emotionally: If the person is trying to get a reaction out of you, remain calm and unemotional. Respond with neutral statements and avoid engaging in drama.

You may explain in these words:

"As a parent, I take my child's medical condition seriously, and I have learned that spanking or punishing is not an effective or safe discipline method for most children. Studies show that it can worsen behavior, especially in children with oppositional defiant disorder. Therefore, I prioritize the following research and seek alternative approaches to discipline, that support my child's well-being. I am grateful that I can give my child the care and attention they need to manage their medical condition successfully. I appreciate your concern."

Or, when others begin discussing punishment for an ODD child, the parent could ask the following question:

"Would you also punish someone with epilepsy? If you would not punish an individual with epilepsy, then you should not punish someone with another neurological disorder like ODD."

Another crucial aspect is educating others about the disorder. This can include sharing resources, such as articles, books, and support groups, that provide information about ODD and its impact on children and families. Parents can also use their experiences to educate others and advocate for their child's needs. For example, if a parent finds that their child benefits from a specific type of therapy, they can share that information with others looking for similar resources.

Advocating for a child's needs is crucial to supporting them through their ODD journey. This can involve advocating for appropriate accommodations and support in school, such as an individualized education plan (IEP). Parents can also support their child's mental health needs by working with healthcare providers to find appropriate treatments and therapies. By advocating for their child, parents can help ensure they have access to the resources and support they need to thrive.

Isolation and loneliness are common experiences when parenting an oppositional defiant disorder child. In many states, children with ODD qualify for respite care, another option worth considering. There are several coping strategies that parents and caregivers can use to help manage the challenges of this disorder:

- One of the most important coping strategies for parents of children with ODD is caring for themselves. It is important to remember that parenting a child with ODD can be very stressful, and it is essential to prioritize your own mental and physical health. This might mean carving out time for self-care activities like exercise, meditation, or hobbies you enjoy. It might also mean seeking support from a mental health professional, like a therapist or counselor, to help you manage your stress and anxiety.

- Another important coping strategy is finding support from others who can recognize and understand what you are going through. This might mean joining a support group for parents of children with ODD or connecting with other parents online. Being able to talk with others who are going through similar challenges can help you feel less isolated and provide you with valuable insights and coping strategies.

- Developing effective coping strategies for managing stress and anxiety related to ODD is also critical. This might involve learning relaxation techniques like deep breathing exercises or mindfulness meditation. It might also involve developing strategies for managing specific ODD behaviors, such as setting clear boundaries and consequences for challenging behavior or using positive reinforcement to encourage desired behaviors. We will discuss these in detail in upcoming chapters.

Finally, parents must practice self-compassion and recognize that coping with ODD is challenging and ongoing. They should celebrate small victories and recognize that progress might be slow and incremental. By focusing on self-care, seeking support from others, and developing effective coping strategies, parents of children with ODD can help manage the challenges of the disorder and provide the best possible support for their child.

Part 2: Discipline Strategies for ODD

Chapter 7:
Basics Skills to Teach Children

Let us talk about self-governing parents first. Self-governing parents emphasize self-governance, or self-rule, in their parenting. They prioritize teaching their children self-control and self-discipline. Self-governing parents emphasize autonomy and independence while setting boundaries and expectations. They encourage polite expression and straightforward communication.

Self-governing parents teach their kids these four abilities:

- Following instructions
- Accepting "No" for an answer
- Accepting consequences
- Disagreeing properly

These four skills can solve 99% of behavioral issues.

You are thinking yes, but my oppositional defiant youngster usually argues back. They will argue poorly. They are disobedient. They will die on that wall. I am aware. Even if you do not think they will use such skills, you must teach them and expect they will. As parents, we must tell our children the truth, which means they need all of the skills and values taught to them, whether they want them or not.

These four basic skills will offer parents something to refer to when the child becomes oppositional.

1. Following Instructions

Oppositional defiant disorder kids may resist following directions. Discipline methods can help:

- Provide clear, basic instructions, breaking them down if required.
- Give children choices within the instructions. That gives them a sense of control.
- Reward children for following directions.
- Convey expectations clearly and consistently to children.

Here is how you discipline a child to obey instructions. You have asked your youngster to clean their room. Your youngster refuses. Several methods may help them follow your instructions:

- Clear instructions: "Put all your clothes in the laundry, pick up all your toys, and make your bed" instead of "Clean your room."
- Offer options: Allow your child to choose within the directions. "Would you like to pick up your toys or make your bed first?"
- Clear expectations: Explain your expectations clearly and consistently to your youngster. For instance, "Cleaning your room before playing with your friends is crucial."
- Reward: Reward your child for following directions. "Excellent job picking up your toys! That truly cleans up your room."

These methods can help your youngster comply and lessen disobedience.

2. Accepting "No" for an Answer

Oppositional defiant disorder kids may fight or get angry when told "No." Discipline methods like the ones below can help:

- Explain: Explain why the youngster cannot have or do something.
- Hold firm: Even if the child argues, stand firm.

- Give options: Provide a child-friendly alternative if possible.
- Reward the child for accepting a "No" without arguing or becoming confrontational.

Here is how to use punishment to help a child accept "No": Let us say your child requests to stay up late to watch a movie on a school night. Your youngster needs sleep for school, so you decide against it. These methods may help your youngster accept your "No":

- Explain: Explain why your child cannot have or do anything. "I know you want to stay up late to watch the movie," you could add.
- Hold firm: Even if your youngster fights, stand firm. "I know you are disappointed, but you need sleep for school," you could say. Watch the movie on the weekend."
- Give options: Try to accommodate your child's wishes. "How about a shorter movie that ends earlier so you can still get enough sleep for school?"
- Reward your youngster for accepting "No" without arguing or becoming confrontational. "I am proud of you for accepting my decision and understanding why school requires appropriate sleep," you could say.

Children with oppositional defiant disorder negotiate everything. Their goal is to explain why they cannot do it. ODD kids often trick their parents into negotiating to sort out the problem and get what they want. Parents who are self-governing do not negotiate with their children. By setting examples and enforcing negative consequences, they set rules and firm boundaries and leave no room for negotiation.

3. Accepting Consequences

Oppositional defiant disorder kids may have trouble accepting the consequences. Discipline methods like the ones below can help:

- Be constant: Be consistent with consequences and let the youngster know what they are.
- Natural consequences: Let the child's actions play out instead of punishing them.
- Apply logic: Require the child to clean up after themselves.
- Reward the youngster when they accept their actions without complaining or becoming violent.

Here is how to assist a child in accepting the consequences through discipline. Let us say your child breached home rules, like staying up late. To assist your youngster in accepting the consequences, try these:

- Explain the consequences: To prepare the child, explain the behavior's repercussions. Say, "If you remain up beyond bedtime, you will forfeit screen time privileges tomorrow."
- Be calm: Keep your cool when enforcing sanctions. This helps your youngster accept penalties without feeling attacked or defensive.
- Show compassion: Empathize with your child yet enforce the consequences. "I know you wanted to stay up late to finish your game, but you broke the rule," you could remark. "You lost tomorrow's screen time."
- Utilize natural consequences as much as possible: A child who refuses to wear a coat will be cold and uncomfortable on a cold day.
- Positive reinforcement: Reward your youngster for accepting punishments without protest. "I'm proud of you for taking responsibility; maturity and accountability," you could say.

4. Disagreeing Appropriately

Oppositional defiant disorder kids may have trouble disagreeing. The discipline methods below can help:

- Communicate properly: Train the child to disagree with "I" statements and avoid blame.
- Clear boundaries: Set boundaries for how the youngster can disagree, such as no disrespectful language or actions.
- Reward the child for respectfully disagreeing.
- Behave properly: Demonstrate respectful disagreement with the youngster.

Here is an example of using discipline to teach a child to disagree. If you are a parent, your child may argue with a decision like not letting them go to a sleepover:

- Promote respectful communication: Teach your youngster to argue politely and calmly. "I understand you are upset about not going to the sleepover," you could say.
- Validate your child's sentiments: Let them know you understand and accept their feelings. "I know you wanted to go to the sleepover, and it is fair to feel disappointed," you could offer.
- Actively listen: Try to grasp your child's perspective. Repeat what you hear to check your understanding. For instance, "So I hear you stating that you want to go to the sleepover because all your buddies will be there."
- Establish boundaries: Stick to your decision and set debate boundaries. "While I understand your perspective, the choice is definitive," for instance. "Let us discuss how to maximize our weekend."
- Promote good behavior: Reward your youngster for respectfully disagreeing. "I appreciate your courteous disagreement."

They can negotiate with you if you educate them on how to disagree. That crucial talent lets them comprehend and be understood.

Oppositional defiant disorder kids have trouble changing the subject. They obsess over the situation's negativity, what they need to control, and who does not understand or care. They push hard because they create drama in their minds. They think they are fighting.

Working with youngsters with real oppositional defiant disorder made me feel compassion for their struggles. That exacerbated their anxiety and tension to such a high level that I believed it must harm their health, so I tried my best to stay cool, teach them the needed skills, and never talk back to them. What do I do if they are still defiant and talking back to me even if I do not? I will say, "You are talking back to me. You are not telling me anything right now. You are only yelling and this is not helping." Remember that oppositional defiant people are lying to themselves. They think everything is a war, but if we are calm—hopefully you are—it does not have to be. It is not a warzone if you are calm. Everything happens inside. They are deceiving themselves that you do not care or comprehend.

Everyone's trying to get them, so we must assist them in recognizing reality by appealing to the prefrontal cortex's reasoning abilities. The simplest approach to start is by describing. Just the truth—no sentiments. The obvious. "Right now, you are pacing," I would say. "You are yelling to tell me something. We cannot talk." I describe their action and would try to correct them by explaining what they should do, what they have earned, and how to practice.

Oppositional defiant disorder kids need consistent correction. They need continuous discipline like any other child to self-regulate. Let me tell you something. Your child with oppositional defiant disorder will fight harder when you try to help them. They continue that also internal discourse. Do not take it personally—it is a habit that will take time to break. ODD is difficult to treat. There are just principles, talents, and proven techniques. Do not forget to seek the aid and skills you need for yourself and them, then constantly follow through, and they will progress even if it is slow at the start. Remember, ODD kids can rewire their brains to overcome defiance.

Empowering the ODD Parenting Community

"Alone we can do so little; together we can do so much." – Helen Keller

The journey of parenting a child with Oppositional Defiant Disorder (ODD) can be isolating and overwhelming at times. As you've been reading this book, perhaps you've found solace in knowing that you're not alone in this journey, and you've started to feel more equipped with tools and strategies to face the challenges ahead.

Many parents, just like you, have been searching for a community that understands and supports their unique experience. They've longed for a resource to help them cope and thrive in the face of adversity. This book aims to be that resource for parents, but it can't reach those who need it without your help.

By leaving a review of this book on Amazon, you'll be contributing to a larger conversation about parenting children with ODD. You'll show other parents that they're part of a strong and supportive community, and you'll introduce them to a resource that can make a significant difference in their lives.

Simply by sharing your personal experience with this book and describing the insights and tools you've gained, you'll be helping other parents feel less alone in their journey. You'll be letting them know that it's possible to build a loving, supportive relationship with their child, despite the challenges that ODD presents.

Moreover, your review will provide hope and encouragement to parents who may be feeling overwhelmed or defeated. By sharing your experience, you'll inspire others to take that first step toward a brighter future for their family.

Thank you so much for your support. Parents of children with ODD deserve understanding, guidance, and camaraderie. Together, we can create a more compassionate and informed community, fostering the growth and well-being of both children and parents alike.

Scan to leave a review

Chapter 8:
Why You Should Avoid Negotiating With Your Children

Children with oppositional defiant disorder often act cruelly and aggressively toward adults, including talking back to them. This behavior can cause arguments at home and make it hard for parents. There may be power struggles and conflict because children with ODD are urged to defy authority and establish independence. This chapter will help you learn how to communicate with an oppositional defiant disorder child and what to do if they respond negatively.

Why Do They Act That Way?

Children with oppositional defiant disorder often negotiate and talk back because they have trouble controlling their emotions and impulses. They may be less tolerant of stress, especially if they feel ignored. A child with ODD may also have trouble reading social cues and understanding others' motivations. They are always trying to convince themselves of false facts in their mind. Life is one big fight for them. Their subconscious tells them that nobody cares or understands them.

Techniques for Communicating With Oppositional Defiant Disorder Kids

A child with oppositional defiant disorder often tries to negotiate out of every situation. These kids would rather want you to accept that they are not going to do as they are told and try to get you into the trap of trying to negotiate with them. This is a bad idea since it weakens your authority as a parent. So train them to argue civilly, and they will be better able to negotiate with you. They can use that crucial skill to try to understand and be understood by you.

Some things to keep in mind before negotiating with them:

- **Maintain Composure and Wait**

Maintaining composure and patience when negotiating with children with oppositional defiant disorder is crucial. Anger and irritation will worsen things and prevent you from finding a solution.

Suppose you are trying to persuade your ODD child to do their homework. Instead of reacting angrily and becoming even more annoyed, you may take a deep breath and explain, "I understand that you are feeling upset, but we must find a way to get your homework done. Is there anything, in particular, preventing you from starting? How can I help you?"

- **Pay Attention to Finding Solutions**

Problem-solving can be more productive than rule-enforcing or disciplining when negotiating with a child with an oppositional defiant disorder. Instead of imposing your order, you should work with them to create a solution that benefits everyone involved.

Let us pretend you are a teacher trying to reason with a student who has ODD and is acting out in class. Just ask the student, "What can we do to ensure that you can engage in class without interrupting the other students?" This approach is preferable to sending them to the principal's office or disciplining them.

- **Be Consistent**

Be explicit and consistent with your expectations and boundaries for your child with oppositional defiant disorder. It can help manage the child's behavior by giving them a sense of structure and predictability.

Your child with ODD may benefit from a firm rule that they must put away their toys before bedtime. Say, "I am sorry, but you did not follow our rule about putting away your toys. So your screen time will be deducted."

- **Encouragement of Good Conduct**

Encourage them when they do well. Children with oppositional defiant disorder frequently have low self-esteem, so boosting their self-esteem and keeping up their good work is crucial.

Imagine you are helping an ODD child who showed composure and controlled their rage. You may congratulate them on using anger management techniques by saying, "I am so proud of you. A lot of courage and determination there."

Get professional assistance from a therapist or counselor specializing in behavior disorders if you are having trouble negotiating with a child with ODD. They can offer individualized assistance and methods for dealing with challenging behaviors.

What to Do if They Talk Back?

Reluctant to change the subject, kids with oppositional defiant disorder are a common phenomenon. They keep ruminating about the people and things that are not helping the issue or the people and things they need to manage. They are so driven by the drama they make in their heads. They imagine themselves to be in the middle of a war zone. Try your best to teach them the skills they need, and make sure you never talk back to them when they are talking back to you. So, what should one do instead?

- Explain Their Action: "Right now, you are talking back to me." "I know you have something to say to me, but you are very stressed and sound like you are yelling." That rules out the possibility of further discussion. It would help if you elaborate on their actions. The final step in correcting someone is to explain what they should do, how much they deserve, and how they can start doing things properly.

- Remain Calm: Do not lose your cool. It is best to keep your cool and not make things worse. Relax and focus on keeping your cool.

- Explain That Their Behavior is Unacceptable: Make it clear to the child that disrespectful communication and talking back are not tolerated. A reasonable response would be, "I know you are furious, but it is not OK to talk to me like that."

- Explain Consequences: Establish and consistently implement consequences for disruptive behavior, such as talking back. This could mean a time-out or the removal of privileges like "Since you have disrespected me, I am taking away your computer time until tomorrow."

- Encourage Problem-Solving: Try encouraging problem-solving and working with them to find a solution instead of punishing them. You could say something like, "Let us talk about it. Is there something bothering you that we can fix?"

Let us explain it with an example:

Parent: "Please put your toys away before dinner."

Child: "I do not want to! Why do you constantly have to force me to do things?"

Parent: "I know you are upset, but speaking to me that way is inappropriate. Respectful discourse is expected from you."

Child: "I refuse."

Parent: "Well, since you argued with me, you will not be able to watch any more TV till tomorrow. But let us discuss what is making you so sad. Is there anything else bothering you at the moment?

Child: "I do not want to."

Parent: "I know you do not want to, but it is really necessary to pick up after yourself. Can we do anything to make it more exciting or less stressful?"

Child: "Well, maybe we could do it together."

Parent: "That is a fantastic plan! Let's work together."

When a child has an oppositional defiant disorder, they will resist even more strongly whenever you try to help them. They try to keep up the pretense of a running monologue there. Do not take it personally; remember, they will need time to break the habit.

Chapter 9:
How to Get a Defiant Child to Obey

Dealing with a stubborn child can be difficult and tiring for parents and caregivers. Frustration and helplessness can occur when a child defies adults and ignores the rules. Remember that resistance is a frequent trait in kids and can be addressed with the correct approaches. This chapter delves into the best practices for communicating with your child, establishing clear boundaries, and encouraging obedience. Whether your child is a toddler or a teenager, these techniques will help you overcome the difficulties of raising a stubborn child and encourage good habits in the long run.

Getting your child to listen might be difficult, but you can take steps to make the process easier. Some ideas are as follows:

- Ensure your child understands your established rules. To ensure that children follow the rules, keep them simple and appropriate for their age. Involve them in setting the rules and explain the consequences of breaking them. Maintain uniformity in applying rules and consequences.

- Use positive reinforcement by praising your child when you see them doing something right. After receiving such praise, they may feel more motivated to maintain their good behavior. We can condemn our kids ten times a day but instead must focus on praising our children ten times a day.

- Give your child the freedom to make some choices and to be independent. Let children pick out their clothes and snacks whenever possible. As a result, they may feel less need to challenge your authority and more confidence in their abilities.

- Provide Consequences. If your child disobeys your rules, take the appropriate action. Ensure the repercussions are fair and suitable for their age, like restricting their screen time.

- Employ a soothing voice and a courteous demeanor when conversing with your child. Be sure to hear them and try to see things from their vantage point.

- A mental health expert can work with you and your kid to establish effective techniques to manage your child's willful conduct if it is chronic or causes substantial concerns.

Here is a story that uses the techniques discussed to motivate a stubborn kid to obey.

Sophie, age 5, is a defiant child who frequently disobeys her mother. Sarah is concerned about her daughter Sophie's disobedience and wants to find ways to get her to comply. Sarah chooses to establish clear boundaries for Sophie, including having her pick up her toys after playing and sticking to her nighttime routine. Sophie will face repercussions if she disobeys, Sarah tells her.

One night, Sarah gently prompts Sophie to put away her toys. Sophie throws a tantrum and continues to reject. Sarah explains to Sophie soothingly that she must pick up her toys or else she will not be allowed to play with them the next day. Sophie keeps sobbing but gradually stops crying and begins gathering her toys. Sarah encourages Sophie to continue to observe the guidelines by praising her for putting away her toys. Sarah congratulates Sophie for doing the right thing, telling her how proud she is of her. Sophie beams with pride at how she has made her mother so happy.

The following day, Sarah inquires what Sophie would want to wear to the park. Sophie picks out a bright pink dress and dresses with enthusiasm. Sophie gets to choose her park snack because of Sarah's flexibility.

Sophie is delighted and confident in her newfound independence. Later that day, Sophie began acting out by throwing sand at other children at the park. It is forbidden to throw sand, so Sarah informs Sophie that they will have to leave the park early if she keeps doing it. Sophie apologizes to the other kids and stops throwing sand at them. On the way out of the park, Sarah converses with Sophie about her flinging sand and explains why that is not okay. She considers Sophie's viewpoint and helps her find more suitable words for expressing herself. Sarah and Sophie feel like they made progress in their chat.

Sophie's defiance has persisted and become increasingly problematic over time. Sarah decides to consult a child therapist about developing methods for dealing with Sophie's disruptive behavior. Sophie grows more cooperative and obedient during therapy as Sarah learns new techniques to help her regulate her feelings and actions.

It is crucial to remember that a child's defiant behavior may be an outward sign of a deeper problem when dealing with them. Defiance can be managed in part by investigating its likely causes. One possible cause of a child's disruptive behavior at school could be anything as simple as a learning deficiency or as serious as bullying. You may be able to help your defiant youngster if you can determine the cause of their behavior and work to correct it.

One method of dealing with disobedience is to wait before imposing consequences. It is easy to react rashly and impose consequences without giving them much thought when tensions are high. Yet, stepping back can help you collect your thoughts and assess the situation more rationally. A more effective punishment that addresses the conduct in question and motivates future improvement can be determined with this information. Taking a break can also help you control your anger, avoid making the problem worse, and strain your relationship with your child. Consider your child's resistance to doing their homework as an example of the situations in which these techniques would be useful. You should probably step back and evaluate the situation before punishing them. You may learn that your kid has been overwhelmed by their schoolwork or has trouble with a specific subject. You can make your child feel more encouraged and motivated to do their schoolwork if you address these underlying concerns. Taking a pause might also help you devise a penalty that effectively addresses the behavior without being too harsh.

A child who throws a tantrum that lasts for hours and refuses to comply may be experiencing developmental delays, anxiety, or other mental health issues. It is best to keep yourself calm and determine why the child acts this way.

To help children overcome their defiant behavior, it is important to teach them proper communication skills to help them convey their needs without being defiant. Parents should use role-playing and positive reinforcement to help children practice good behavior. Nobody can deny praising children, which is essential for an attitude shift. Remain calm and positive while teaching and correcting your children.

Chapter 10:
How to Discipline a Teenager That Will Not Listen

Disciplining a teenager who will not listen is a common challenge many parents face. Failure to address this issue can significantly affect the teenager and the family. Adolescence changes the brain significantly, making teenagers more impulsive, reactive, and sensitive to stress and conflict. Understanding these changes is crucial when disciplining them. Effective discipline includes effective communication, setting limits and boundaries, and seeking professional help when necessary. Being patient, consistent, and compassionate when disciplining a teenager who will not listen is crucial. Parents should seek support from friends, family, and professionals when facing this challenge. Teenage disobedience can stem from various factors, including peer pressure, a lack of respect for authority, a desire for independence, and underlying emotional and psychological issues. Identifying the root cause of teenage disobedience is critical when developing a discipline strategy.

There are various strategies parents can use when disciplining a teenager. Three common strategies include positive reinforcement, natural consequences, and logical consequences. Each strategy has its benefits and limitations, and the choice of strategy depends on the specific situation and the teenager's needs.

- Positive Reinforcement: Positive reinforcement involves rewarding a teenager for good behavior. Rewards can be verbal praise, privileges, or tangible rewards such as gifts or allowances. Teenagers can repeat positive behavior when they receive positive reinforcement.

- Natural Consequences: Natural consequences involve allowing teenagers to experience the natural outcome of their behavior without intervening. For example, a teenager who does not study for an exam may receive a poor grade.

- Logical Consequences: Logical consequences are consequences logically related to the misbehavior. For example, if teenagers break curfew, they may lose the privilege of hanging out with friends on the weekends.

Effective communication is critical when disciplining a teenager who does not listen. It can help parents understand their teenager's perspective, feelings, and needs, which promotes mutual understanding and respect. Moreover, it allows parents to communicate their expectations and consequences clearly and understandably to their teenagers. Active listening is crucial to effective communication. It involves listening attentively to teenagers' concerns, emotions, and needs without interrupting or judging them. Active listening can help parents build trust, validate teenagers' feelings, and promote open and honest communication.

Here are some suggestions for communicating effectively with a teenager who will not listen:

- Choose the right time and place: Choose a time and place where you and your teenager can communicate without distractions or interruptions.

- Listen actively: Listen to your teenager's perspective and emotions without interrupting or judging them. Restate what you heard to ensure you understand their perspective.

- Use "I" statements: Use "I" statements to express your feelings about the behavior or situation without blaming or attacking your teenager.

- Be clear and specific: Be precise about your expectations and disobedience consequences. Use clear and easy-to-understand language.

- Avoid criticism: Avoid criticizing or blaming your teenager for their behavior. Instead, focus on the behavior and the consequences.
- Encourage participation: Encourage your teenager to participate in the conversation and express their thoughts and feelings.
- End on a positive note: End the conversation positively, emphasizing your love and support for your teenager.

Setting limits and boundaries is essential when disciplining a teenager who will not listen. Limits and boundaries provide structure and guidance for teenagers, helping them understand what is expected of them and what behavior is acceptable. Clear limits and boundaries can help parents prevent conflict, establish authority, and promote healthy family relationships.

Being consistent and firm when enforcing these boundaries is crucial. Teenagers not held accountable for their actions may develop a sense of entitlement and feel they can get away with disobedience. In contrast, consistent and firm boundary enforcement can promote accountability, responsibility, and respect for authority.

Here are some examples of setting effective limits and boundaries:

- Establish household rules: Establish clear, specific, and easy-to-understand household rules. For example, rules might include curfews, phone or internet usage limits, and expectations around chores and homework.
- Set consequences for disobedience: Set clear and consistent consequences for disobedience. Consequences might include loss of privileges, extra chores, or temporary loss of phone or internet access.
- Be firm and consistent: Be firm and consistent when enforcing these rules and consequences. Make sure your teenager

understands the expectations and consequences of disobedience.

- Involve your teenager in setting boundaries: Involve your teenager in setting boundaries and consequences. This can help them understand the reasons behind the rules and consequences and promote ownership and responsibility.

- Be willing to compromise: Be willing to compromise and negotiate when appropriate. For example, if your teenager wants to stay out later than the established curfew, you might be able to adjust the curfew under certain circumstances.

- Monitor and adjust: Monitor your teenager's behavior and adjust boundaries and consequences as necessary. As your teenager grows and develops, their needs and behaviors may change, and your discipline approach may need to adapt accordingly.

If a teenager's disobedience is severe or persistent, it may be essential to seek professional help. Professional help can provide additional resources and support that can help address the underlying issues that may contribute to disobedience.

Finding the right professional can be challenging, but here are some tips to help:

- Ask for recommendations: Ask for recommendations from trusted friends, family, or healthcare professionals.

- Research: Research potential professionals and look for those with expertise in your specific issue.

- Consider their approach: Consider their approach to treatment and philosophy. Look for professionals who align with your values and goals.

- Check credentials: Check the professional's credentials, including education, training, and licensing.

- Meet with the professional: Meet with the professional before treating. Use this meeting to ask questions, learn more about their approach, and determine if they fit appropriately.

Once you have found a professional, it is essential to work effectively with them to promote positive outcomes. Here are some tips to help you:

- Be open and honest: Be open and honest with the professional about your concerns, goals, and expectations.

- Follow their recommendations: Follow the professional's recommendations, including treatment options and homework assignments.

- Make sure you attend appointments regularly and discuss progress and challenges.

- Involve the teenager: Involve the teenager in the process as much as possible, including attending appointments and participating in treatment.

- Stay positive and patient: Stay positive and patient throughout the treatment process. Change takes time, and progress may not be immediate.

Discipline strategies, including positive reinforcement and natural and logical consequences, can be beneficial when tailored to the specific situation and the teenager's needs. Effective communication, setting limits and boundaries, and seeking professional help when necessary are also essential components of effective discipline.

When disciplining a teenager, being patient, consistent, and compassionate is crucial. Parents should also seek support from friends, family, and professionals when facing this challenge. By following these strategies and seeking support, parents can promote their teenager's healthy development and strengthen their relationship with them when necessary.

Chapter 11:
How to Deal With Teenage Temper Tantrums

Teenage tantrums can be overwhelming and frustrating for parents and caregivers. Adolescents struggle through a significant transition, and tantrums can be a natural part of their emotional development. However, parents and caregivers must know how to manage these tantrums effectively to prevent regular occurrences. In this chapter, we will explore the causes of teenage tantrums and provide practical tips for managing them. This chapter will help you understand how to help teenagers healthily navigate their emotions.

Possible Causes of Teenage Tantrums

There are several causes of teenage tantrums, and it is imperative to understand these underlying factors to manage and prevent them effectively. Here are some common causes of teenage tantrums:

1. **Hormonal Changes**

   Teenagers undergo significant hormonal changes during puberty, which can lead to mood swings and emotional outbursts.

2. **Stress and Anxiety**

   Teenagers face many stressors, such as academic pressure, social anxiety, and family conflicts, which can trigger tantrums.

3. **Lack of Emotional Regulation Skills**

   Adolescents are still developing their emotional regulation skills and may not know how to express their feelings effectively.

4. **Wanting Independence**

   As teenagers strive for independence, they may become frustrated when their parents or caregivers are not giving them enough freedom.

5. **Physical Discomfort or Illness**

   Physical discomfort or illness can also trigger teenage tantrums. Chronic pain or chronic illness can cause mood swings and emotional outbursts.

Every child is unique and may have different causes for tantrums. By identifying the underlying causes of tantrums, parents and caregivers can help teenagers manage their emotions better. Teenage temper tantrums can be challenging for parents, caregivers, and teachers. However, with the right approach and techniques, teenagers can overcome their tantrums and emotional outbursts

Tip #1: Teach Calmness

The first step in dealing with temper tantrums is teaching teenagers to be calm. This involves teaching them to recognize and manage their emotions. It is worthwhile to explain what calm means and how to achieve it. They need to know that calmness is a decision they can make in the prefrontal cortex of their brain. This means that even when they feel emotional, they can stop being emotional and calm down instead of escalating the situation further.

Teaching teenagers to be calm requires deliberate effort and consistency. Parents and caregivers need to reinforce calmness by modeling calm behavior themselves. It is also helpful to provide teenagers with cues that indicate they are getting emotional. This is so they can recognize when to step back and relax.

Tip #2: Teach Them How to Express Themselves

Tantruming has become a habit or skill for teenagers. Teaching them other skills to express themselves is essential to overcome this.

Teenagers are frustrated because they cannot attend a party with their friends. Instead of throwing a tantrum, you can help them express themselves positively by following these steps:

- Start by acknowledging their feelings and showing empathy. Say something like, "I understand you are disappointed about missing the party."

- Encourage teenagers to express themselves positively. Ask them what they feel and why they want to attend the party.

- Work together to find a solution that satisfies the teenager and the parent. For example, if the parent is concerned about the child's safety, they can suggest an alternative activity with friends with which both parties are comfortable.

- Engage the teenager in role-playing scenarios to practice positive communication. Help them use "I" statements instead of blaming or attacking language. For example, instead of saying, "You never let me do anything!" they can say, "I feel frustrated when I am unable to do things with my friends."

Teaching teenagers these skills is not a one-time thing; it requires practice and consistency. Parents and caregivers should be understanding and supportive as teenagers learn and implement these skills daily.

Tip #3: Have a Plan to Correct Them

Having a plan to correct teenagers when they exhibit out-of-control behavior is imperative. This involves setting clear boundaries and expectations and communicating consequences in advance. Parents and caregivers should also have a script for correcting teenagers so they know exactly what to expect.

The key to this approach is consistency. Teenagers must know that their actions have consequences, and parents and caregivers must follow through with any disciplinary action they promise.

Tip #4: Learn to Calm Yourself

The most effective way to help teenagers overcome temper tantrums is to model calm behavior yourself. As Nicholeen Peck, a parenting expert, suggests, "If you want to conquer teenage temper tantrums, you have got to conquer your temper tantrums too."

Parents and caregivers must work on their emotional regulation and model calmness. This means remaining calm and collected even in challenging situations. When parents and caregivers are calm, they can respond to teenagers' emotional outbursts more helpfully and productively.

Here are some additional tips for managing teenage tantrums:

- Validate their feelings: When a teenager has a tantrum, validating their feelings is worthwhile, even if you disagree with their behavior. This means recognizing and accepting their emotions and letting them know you understand their feelings.

- Encourage problem-solving: Instead of getting into a power struggle with a teenager during a tantrum, encourage problem-solving. Ask them what they think could solve the problem and work together to find a solution.

- Take a break: Sometimes, it is more appropriate to return to the issue later when everyone is calmer. This can help everyone cool down and approach the problem more clearly.

- Set boundaries and consequences: Ensure teenagers understand their behavior's boundaries and consequences. Be clear about what is and is not acceptable and the consequences if they continue their tantrums.

- Praise positive behavior: When teenagers calm themselves down or use their problem-solving skills, praise them for their positive behavior. This can reinforce those skills and encourage them to use them.

- Seek professional help if needed: If a teenager's tantrums are frequent or severe, seeking a mental health professional may be helpful. They can work with the teenager and family to develop strategies for managing emotions and behaviors.

Dealing with teenage temper tantrums can be challenging. However, with the right approach, parents and caregivers can help teenagers overcome their emotional outbursts and develop the skills to express themselves effectively.

Chapter 12:
How to Teach a Child Respect and Discipline

Respect and discipline are two essential components of child development. They play a crucial role in shaping a child's behavior and character, helping them become responsible and productive members of society. Respect is the foundation of positive relationships, essential for healthy emotional and social development. Children develop a positive self-image and empathy when they learn to respect themselves and others. Respect teaches children to value diversity and appreciate differences, a crucial aspect of their personal growth and development.

Discipline, on the other hand, provides structure and guidance for child behavior. It helps them understand the consequences of their actions and learn to take responsibility for their behavior. Discipline teaches children key life skills such as self-control, problem-solving, and decision-making. By teaching children the value of discipline, we help them develop self-esteem, self-confidence, and independence.

Respect and discipline are significant in a child's development for several reasons. First, they help children develop social and emotional skills essential for healthy relationships and successful communication. Children who learn to respect others and follow the rules are more likely to interact positively with peers, teachers, and family members. They also learn to regulate emotions, handle stress, and make wise decisions. Secondly, respect and discipline teach children key life skills such as responsibility, accountability, and self-discipline. These skills can help children achieve academic and personal success and navigate challenges and obstacles in life.

However, there are some common misconceptions about respect and discipline. Some believe discipline involves punishment and authoritarian control, while respect involves blind obedience and conformity. This is not true. Discipline should be used to teach children to take responsibility for their behavior, understand the consequences of their actions, and make positive choices. Respect should be shown toward individuals for who they are, regardless of their behavior or actions.

Setting Clear Expectations

Setting clear expectations for behavior is essential to teaching children respect and discipline. To achieve this, it is imperative to communicate expectations clearly and specifically. This involves including the child in the process and enforcing them firmly. It is crucial to reinforce expectations consistently and avoid exceptions. Additionally, consistent consequences for actions are imperative to teach children that their behavior has consequences. Consequences should be clear, immediate, and equitable across all situations and applied fairly to all children. By setting clear expectations and consistent consequences, children can develop a clear understanding of appropriate behavior and the consequences of their actions.

Understanding and Respecting Boundaries

Teaching children to understand and respect boundaries is crucial to respect and discipline. To do so, it is essential to be clear and specific about boundaries and their reasons. It is also important to reinforce them and encourage respect for others' boundaries. By teaching children to communicate their boundaries respectfully and respect others' boundaries, they can develop key social and emotional skills.

Influence of Adult Behavior on Children

Children learn by observing the adults around them, and adult behavior significantly impacts children's behavior. Adults who model respectful and disciplined behavior can positively influence children's behavior, while those who model negative behavior, such as aggression or disrespect, can have a negative impact. Adult communication style also significantly affects how children learn to communicate. Adults who communicate respectfully and positively can encourage children to do the same. In contrast, those who behave aggressively or disrespectfully can lead children to do the same. Lastly, adults who consistently follow the rules and demonstrate an understanding of consequences can help children understand the importance of rules and discipline.

In contrast, those who consistently break the rules or lack an understanding of consequences can undermine these values. Therefore, adults should model positive behavior and attitudes toward respect and discipline to promote children's development. It is also important to consistently enforce them and encourage respect for others' boundaries. This can help children develop critical social and emotional skills, such as communication and empathy.

Modeling Respectful Behavior

Modeling respectful behavior is crucial to teaching children respect and discipline. Adults can use various strategies such as effective and appropriate communication, positive reinforcement, active listening, avoiding aggressive behavior, and using conflict resolution strategies to model respectful behavior. Creating a positive and constructive environment is also important. This can be achieved by setting clear expectations for behavior, encouraging appropriate behavior through reinforcement, setting examples of respectful behavior toward diversity, and encouraging communication and problem-solving skills.

Effective Communication Strategies

Effective communication strategies are essential for disciplining children. It is crucial to avoid yelling, shame, or physical punishment. Instead, focus on teaching children the consequences of their behavior, taking responsibility for their actions, and making wise choices in the future. Effective communication strategies for disciplining children include being clear and direct, staying calm and respectful, using active listening, and using positive reinforcement and praise. Adults can use these strategies to help children navigate challenges and build positive relationships.

Active listening is a crucial communication strategy in disciplining children, as it helps them feel heard and understood. Adults can actively listen by giving their full attention, showing empathy, and validating their child's feelings. Positive reinforcement and praise are also effective strategies for disciplining children, and adults should be specific and consistent and use non-material rewards.

Age-Appropriate Strategies

Discipline strategies should also be age-appropriate to teach children respect and discipline effectively. For toddlers and preschoolers, redirecting their attention and providing positive reinforcement can be effective. For school-aged children, time-outs, loss of privileges, and logical consequences can be effective. Adolescents are more autonomous than adults, and involving them in creating expectations and consequences can be beneficial. Consequences should be related to the behavior and not involve shaming or punishment.

Encourage Positive Reinforcement

Positive reinforcement, natural consequences, and restitution are some positive discipline techniques. Positive reinforcement involves praising and rewarding appropriate behavior, while natural consequences allow children to experience their consequences. Restitution involves encouraging children to make amends for their behavior. Encouraging positive behavior through reinforcement is also helpful in teaching respect and discipline. Adults can be specific about the behavior they are reinforcing, consistently reinforce positive behavior, and look for natural opportunities to reinforce positive behavior.

Teach Children to Be Responsible

Teaching children to take responsibility for their behavior is crucial to teaching respect and discipline. Adults can help children take responsibility by acknowledging the behavior that needs to change. They can also encourage self-reflection, setting clear expectations, and consistently enforcing consequences. Encouraging self-reflection and problem-solving skills is also very beneficial, and adults can do this by asking open-ended questions, providing guidance and support, and encouraging creativity. Helping children develop self-discipline through positive reinforcement is equally imperative, and adults can do this by praising effort, rewarding positive behavior, and focusing on progress. By using these strategies, adults can assist children in developing the skills they need to make positive choices and navigate challenges in life.

Teaching respect and discipline to children is necessary for their development and success. By using effective communication strategies, age-appropriate discipline techniques, and positive reinforcement, parents can help children develop the social and emotional skills they need to navigate life's challenges and build meaningful relationships. Parents can set children up for success and a fulfilling life by consistently modeling respectful behavior and creating a positive environment.

Chapter 13:
How to Get Kids to Go to Bed

Getting enough sleep is crucial for everyone, but especially for kids who are still growing and developing. Studies show adequate sleep can boost physical and mental health, academic performance, and overall well-being. However, as any parent knows, getting kids to bed and staying there can be a major challenge. This can lead to sleep deprivation, negatively affecting behavior, mood, and cognitive function. Every child is unique, and what works for one child may not work for another. However, by implementing some of the strategies discussed in this chapter, parents can increase their chances of success in helping their children get the sleep they need. Let us dive in and explore how to get kids to go to bed.

To help kids establish healthy sleep habits, it is a must to understand their sleep needs. Kids' sleep requirements vary based on age, developmental stage, and individual needs. The American Academy of Sleep Medicine (AASM) provides the following guidelines for recommended sleep hours by age group:

- Infants (4-12 months): 12-16 hours
- Toddlers (1-2 years): 11-14 hours
- Preschoolers (3-5 years): 10-13 hours
- School-age children (6-12 years): 9-12 hours
- Teenagers (13-18 years): 8-10 hours

These are general guidelines; some children may need more sleep than recommended.

Many children struggle with sleep problems despite their parents' best efforts. Some common sleep problems in kids include difficulty falling asleep, nighttime awakenings, early waking, snoring and sleep apnea, nightmares and night terrors, restless legs syndrome, sleepwalking, and sleep talking. Sleep problems can have a variety of causes, including medical conditions, stress, anxiety, environmental factors, and poor sleep habits. Identifying the underlying cause of sleep problems is crucial in developing effective strategies to address them. By seeking medical help, addressing environmental factors, implementing healthy sleep habits, and using relaxation techniques, parents can help their children establish healthy sleep habits and patterns. This will promote restful and restorative sleep.

Creating a Bedtime Routine

A consistent bedtime routine can help children transition from waking hours to sleep. A bedtime routine provides structure and predictability, signaling the child that it is time to wind down and prepare for sleep. Establishing a bedtime routine for children provides numerous benefits. These include reducing anxiety and stress that interferes with sleep. They also help the child feel more secure and calm. This is done by encouraging healthy sleep habits and patterns, promoting parent-child bonding, and encouraging the child to develop independence and self-regulation skills.

Bedtime routine components should be customized based on the child's age, interests, and needs. However, some common components of an effective bedtime routine include a consistent bedtime and wake-up time, winding down activities such as reading, listening to calming music, taking a warm bath, dimming lights, minimizing noise, putting on comfortable sleep clothes, brushing teeth and using the bathroom, and a bedtime story or conversation with a parent. It is imperative to avoid stimulating activities or electronics before bedtime, as they can interfere with the child's sleep.

Tips for Sticking to a Bedtime Routine

Establishing a consistent bedtime routine can take time and effort, but some tips can make it easier, including:

- Start the bedtime routine at the same time each night.
- Be consistent with the routine, even on weekends or during vacations.
- Involve the child in the routine allowing them to choose some components.
- Provide gentle reminders and encouragement to follow the routine.
- Adjust the routine as needed but avoid major changes too frequently.

Setting the Right Sleep Environment

Sleep environments can significantly impact a child's ability to fall and stay asleep. Creating a calm, relaxing, supportive environment can promote healthy sleep habits and patterns. A comfortable sleep environment is essential for a child to get the rest they need. A comfortable sleep environment should be quiet, cool, and distraction-free. A quality mattress and pillows are also needed for a good night's sleep.

Some tips for creating a sleep-friendly environment include:

- Make sure the room is cool and well-ventilated.
- Use blackout curtains or shades to keep the room dark.
- Use white noise or a sound machine to block out external noise.
- Remove electronic devices from the bedroom or turn them off completely.
- Ensure the mattress and pillows are comfortable and supportive.

Children may experience sleep disruptions, including nightmares, fears, and physical discomfort. Some tips for addressing these disruptions include:

- Encourage the child to talk about their fears or concerns before bedtime.
- Provide a night light or flashlight if the child is afraid of the dark.
- Address any physical discomfort such as hunger, thirst, or discomfort with clothing or bedding.
- Address any underlying medical or psychological issues that may cause sleep disruptions.
- Be patient and supportive and offer comfort and reassurance when needed.

Parents can help their children establish healthy sleep habits and patterns that promote restful and restorative sleep. This is done by creating a sleep-friendly environment that addresses potential sleep disruptions.

Handling Resistance and Behavioral Challenges

Children may resist putting themselves to bed despite a consistent bedtime routine and a supportive sleep environment. Understanding common reasons kids resist bedtime and implementing strategies for dealing with resistance and challenging behavior can help parents establish healthy sleep habits for their children.

Some common reasons why kids resist bedtime include:

- Fear of missing out on activities or events
- Separation anxiety
- Resistance to routine changes
- Difficulty transitioning from waking hours to sleep time
- Overstimulation from electronic devices or activities
- Hunger or thirst

Some strategies for dealing with resistance and challenging behavior include:

- Set clear and consistent rules and consequences for not following the bedtime routine.
- Provide choices within the bedtime routine to give the child control.
- Establish a reward system for following the bedtime routine.
- Use calming techniques such as deep breathing or visualization.
- Engage the child in relaxation activities, such as reading or listening to calming music.

Parents can help their children develop healthy sleep habits and patterns by using positive reinforcement, consequences, and communication techniques.

Supporting Good Sleep Habits

Establishing healthy sleep habits involves more than creating a consistent bedtime routine and a sleep-friendly environment. A child's diet, exercise routine, and daytime activities can also impact their ability to get the rest they need. A good diet and regular exercise can contribute to healthy sleep habits.

Some tips for promoting sound sleep through diet and exercise include:

- Encourage regular physical activity, especially in the morning or early afternoon.
- Avoid heavy meals or snacks before bedtime.
- Encourage consumption of foods containing sleep-promoting nutrients, such as magnesium, tryptophan, and melatonin.

- Limit caffeine intake, especially in the afternoon and evening.

Screen time can significantly impact a child's ability to fall and stay asleep.

Some tips for using screen time effectively include:

- Avoid screen time for at least an hour before bedtime.
- Set limits on screen time during the day.
- Encourage screen time for educational or relaxing activities rather than stimulating or exciting activities.
- Use apps or features that adjust screen brightness and color temperature to reduce sleep impact.

By promoting healthy sleep habits through diet, exercise, daytime activities, and screen time, parents can help their children establish healthy sleep habits and patterns. This will promote restful and restorative sleep.

Troubleshooting Sleep Problems

Even with the best efforts to establish healthy sleep habits, children may still experience sleep problems. Understanding when to seek help for persistent sleep problems, identifying common sleep disorders and their signs, and implementing strategies for addressing sleep issues can help parents promote restful and restorative sleep for their children.

Parents should seek medical help if their child consistently experiences sleep problems such as difficulty falling asleep, frequent night awakenings, or excessive daytime sleepiness. Sleep problems can indicate an underlying medical or psychological issue that requires professional attention.

Many sleep disorders affect children, including:

- Sleep apnea: Breathing difficulties during sleep that can lead to frequent night awakenings and daytime sleepiness
- Insomnia: Difficulty falling asleep or staying asleep
- Restless leg syndrome: An uncomfortable sensation in the legs that interferes with sleep
- Narcolepsy: Excessive daytime sleepiness and sudden sleep attacks
- Parasomnias: Sleepwalking, night terrors, and other unusual sleep behaviors

Parents should talk to their child's healthcare provider if they suspect their child is experiencing a sleep disorder. Parents can help their children establish healthy sleep habits and patterns that promote restful and restorative sleep by identifying and addressing sleep problems.

Establishing healthy sleep habits for children is incredibly beneficial for their health and well-being. By understanding children's sleep needs, creating a bedtime routine and sleep-friendly environment, promoting healthy habits during the day, and addressing sleep problems, parents can help their children get the restful and restorative sleep they need.

Chapter 14:
How to Stop Your Kid From Talking Back

Let us discuss how to stop your kid from talking back. In this chapter, I aim to explain some key skills you can teach your children; skills they can use to be understood without talking back and showing disrespect.

Remember, when your child talks back, they do not know another way to get heard. When your child talks back to you, do not respond.

If they say, "You do not care about me," do not say, "Oh yes, I do, honey, I care about you." They are trying to start a power struggle. If you engage and fight back with them, you will get sucked into that power struggle going back and forth and getting nowhere. So, a key thing to remember if your child talks back is not to talk back to them. Instead, say, "I can tell you want to tell me something. I want to know what you have to say right now. But we have got to be calm first, and then we can talk about it."

There is a very valuable skill called "disagreeing appropriately" which is not only useful for parents but for children as well.

Disagreeing appropriately has seven steps. Those steps are:

1. Look at the person.
2. Keep a calm face, voice, and body.
3. Say that you understand their point of view.
4. Share your point of view.
5. Listen to what they have to say.
6. Say okay.

7. Drop the subject.

When a child learns to disagree appropriately, they can express it calmly and respectfully. For instance, they might look at you with a composed face, voice, and body and say, "Mom, may I disagree appropriately?" Then, you would respond with a "Yes" unless they have already disagreed appropriately about the same issue.

After that, the child would acknowledge their point of view and say, "Mom, I understand that you do not want me to have a piece of cake because it is almost dinner time." This shows that they understand your perspective. Next, they would share their point of view by saying, "But that is a piece of cake I was going to have at lunch, and it is my last piece of birthday cake. I saved it until I was a little hungry, and I am hungry now. Can I eat it now? Since it is the only piece I would have had this whole day." At this point, as a parent, you get to decide whether to allow the child to have the cake or not. Regardless of your decision, the child must accept it graciously. If you say "No," the child should accept that without argument. If you say "Yes," you might want to praise your child for using disagreement skills appropriately. For example, you could say, "That is a great disagreement. You showed wonderful self-government. Yes, you can have your cake before dinner. But save room because we are having your favorite tacos tonight."

I hope this example helps illustrate the importance of teaching children to disagree appropriately. It can lead to more productive and respectful communication in families and other relationships.

When a child disagrees appropriately, they choose not to complain or have an attitude problem. They are not going to the emotional part of their brain. They are going to the pre-frontal cortex, the logical part of their brain. They are sorting out all the information and planning what needs to be done to speak with the individual. That is self-government. The child will see that disagreeing appropriately and reaching the pre-frontal cortex gets them more of what they want than talking back and engaging in a power struggle does. They soon realize that the skill of disagreeing appropriately is an excellent one, and this one skill opens the door for using all of the other skills like problem-solving, critical thinking, and impulse control. It also helps them develop interpersonal skills, such as empathy and communication.

So, what if you teach your child to disagree appropriately, and they still talk back? That could happen. If you want to know how to correct them, you need to know the expectation trap versus the cycle for success.

There are five steps to disciplining a child who talks back at you:

1. Before your children talk back to you, plan. If you want to correct them effectively, prepare them for what is to come. Effective correction involves describing what went wrong, providing a rationale, highlighting what went right, and rewarding them. This is followed by practicing the right way to do things through role-play and allowing them to earn extra chores. By doing this, you are teaching them that work is the antidote for sickness. Finally, they check back and drop the subject because they know that is what they have to do if they do not disagree appropriately.

    If your child talks to you in a way that is not calm and composed, even if they are trying to disagree appropriately, you will need to correct that behavior. For instance, if your child says, "Can I disagree appropriately?" and you say, "Yes," but then they say, "Mom, I understand that you do not want me to go outside and play after dinner. But I told Johnny that I would come," you can explain that you know they want to go, but you still need to say "No." This is another opportunity to teach them the skill of accepting a "No" answer. If they continue to argue, they are not dropping the subject, and you will need to correct that behavior. During practice, emphasize the importance of dropping the subject and how it can benefit them.

2. I wanted to share another important pre-teaching strategy you can use with your children. It is called PREP, and it is done right when they need to practice using a particular skill set. For example, if you are about to give them a "No" answer, you can use PREP to teach them how to accept it. You ask them if they remember how to accept a "No" answer. If they say "Yes," you can ask them to tell you the steps. If they need a reminder, you can tell them to look at the person, keep a calm face, voice, and body, say okay, or ask to disagree appropriately, and then drop the subject.

3. Next, you can give them the "No" answer and say, "No, you cannot go out and play with John right now, OK?" This preps their brain to use the right skill set in response to the situation. When they say "OK," you can praise them for doing that.

   It may seem strange to tell someone exactly what you will do right before you do it. However, this type of pre-teaching can work wonders for the brain. By prepping them now, you are setting them up for success and helping them build critical skills to benefit them.

4. When your child talks back to you inappropriately, correcting them using the strategy of disagreement appropriately is critical. If they do not use this skill and talk back to you, you should not talk back to them in return. Instead, you can start correcting them by calmly explaining what they did wrong.

   For example, you could say, "Just now, I gave you a 'No' answer, and you looked at me, but you did not keep a calm face, voice, or body." It is essential to describe what they did wrong instead of reacting and correcting them with a calm tone. A good correction involves telling them what they did, what they should have done, why it was the wrong idea, what they should do in the future, and maybe why it is a good idea. Afterward, you can have them practice doing it correctly and accept the consequences.

They must turn their hearts toward you during the correction process. Correcting your child should be a bonding moment, not a moment where they feel like they did something wrong. To avoid taking them personally, we need to be OK with the wrong or even bad choices they make. Children tend to accept their choices even tighter when people take things personally. We can help them develop better skills and behaviors by creating a safe space for them to correct their behavior.

5. Praising your child when they demonstrate positive behavior by disagreeing appropriately is very worthwhile. If your child takes a moment to disengage their emotional brain and engage their logical processing, which is their pre-frontal cortex, they make a huge move and a wise choice. At that moment, they will have communicated calmly and respectfully with you. It is worthwhile to acknowledge and praise them for it.

If you want to teach your child self-government, they must learn cause and effect. This means that when they do something good, they should feel positive. Praising them for using the right skills will show them they have made the right choice. When you praise them, do not just do it with emotion, but also describe what happened right. This type of praise is the most effective kind they can receive, and it will help them develop the right skills and behaviors for the future.

For example, if your child wants something minor like another cookie or more playtime and asks to disagree appropriately by saying, "Mom, may I disagree appropriately?" you can say "Yes," and let them have the last cookie or more playtime. By agreeing with them, you show them that disagreeing properly works and is a useful way to communicate with you. When they see that this skill is effective, they are more likely to use it in the future.

6. To encourage your child to use the skill of disagreeing appropriately in the future, it is also important to see their perspective. By trying to understand your child's perspective, you put yourself in their shoes and try to understand how they feel and think. Understanding why they might disagree with you helps you appreciate their viewpoint. Seeing their perspective will allow you to choose a response acknowledging their thoughts and feelings, encouraging them to communicate with you more openly and respectfully. Making decisions based on their opinions and feelings shows that you value them.

Now, there is a warning.

Children taught how to disagree appropriately will quickly realize that it works, except for the oppositional defiant ones who do not want to stop being emotional and hate the skill. But you have to teach them to use it anyway. They disagree about everything, and some parents can get pretty frustrated with that. But do not let yourself down. Just remember that disagreeing appropriately is also accepting a "No" answer.

Chapter 15:
How to Punish a Child for Bad Behavior

If someone asks me how to punish a child for bad behavior, I do not use the word "punish" because it usually means getting revenge or vindictive. Correcting bad behavior is necessary, but it is important to approach it in a way that is not emotional or vengeful. Instead, focus on teaching children self-government.

Self-government is about analyzing oneself, planning for the future, and deliberately acting on those plans. It is about understanding cause and effect and controlling one's behavior. When children learn about self-government, they learn that good behavior leads to good outcomes, and bad behavior leads to negative consequences.

Unfortunately, some people use manipulative tactics like hitting, yelling, or giving the silent treatment, which can cause fear and intimidation. These tactics are not effective in teaching self-government. To truly change a child's behavior, we need to approach them with honesty and a desire to help them change their hearts. Self-government is a process of changing hearts and learning to make better choices. So, instead of punishing children, we must focus on teaching them self-government skills and helping them understand the importance of making positive choices.

When correcting behavior, do not use punishments, but use consequences. The difference is that consequences are predetermined and follow through with what was already discussed, while punishments are often used for intimidation. For example, instead of counting to three and using manipulation, we teach children to follow instructions and give them specific steps. If they choose not to follow the instructions, we do a correction, which includes earning an extra chore.

According to Samuel Smiles, a British author and government reformer, this consequence is based on the idea that work is the antidote for a sick character. This type of consequence is something that they can accept and is not imposed in a dominating way. We tell them the extra chore and expect them to do it without complaining or pouting. The goal is to help children accept responsibility for their actions and learn to make positive choices without punishment. Extra chores are quick repentance. They are not things that follow them all day, like losing certain privileges or taking certain things away from them. They are quick things. They can shift and move on, which is what they need to do.

Let me explain this with an example. Through this example, I hope you can notice how different it is from punishing them. You need to notice how I use words such as "You earned" and "You chose." I also want you to pay attention to how I help them know how to say what is right before I even correct them. Suppose you asked your child to throw away the trash, and he ignored you because he wanted to play with his friends right now. Start with pre-teaching to remind them of the skill they already know and how to accept a consequence. And tell them, "Right now, we will have a corrective teaching moment. Do you remember how to accept a consequence?" Then they will say "Yes." You will reply "Great. What are the steps to accepting a consequence?" And they will tell you those steps. Then praise them and say, "Great job. You understand how to cope with a consequence." Here is the correction: "Just a few minutes ago, I gave you an instruction to take the trash out, and you walked away from me when I gave that instruction. That means you did not look at me. You did not maintain a calm face, voice, or body. You did not do the task immediately or check back. You did not follow the instructions. "

And after you do that, have another conversation about trash. It would be best if you had looked at the child, kept a calm voice, and said OK or asked to disagree appropriately. "Do the task immediately and check back. Since you chose not to do those five steps in the following instructions, you earned an extra chore, OK? " At that point, they say, "OK." Then praise them, "You did a great job keeping a calm face, voice, and body and saying OK. I know you are choosing to accept a correction right now. A negative consequence would take longer, and you would want to return to play. But you are making the right choice. You can wash out the kitchen sink for your extra chore, OK?" They will reply, "OK." Then praise them.

Parents can also practice doing things the right way. They can do roleplay practices with the child of following instructions before the real event. Then, when the child gets to take out the trash and wash the kitchen sink, check back for both those things and praise them. Tell them they did a great job, and then they get to move on to play with their friends like they wanted to in the first place, which was why they walked away from you when you tried to tell them to take out the trash.

This type of correction is different from punishment. It touches the person's heart and mind. By taking responsibility for their behavior, they can choose different behavior.

Chapter 16:
How to Teach a Kid Not to Hit

Children are most likely to hit when young, but it can happen at any age. It seems that they develop other methods for power struggles or control situations as they age. The same rules apply regardless of whether your child is younger or older. This chapter will provide you with some helpful information.

So why do children hit? It is important to start there.

It is usually because a child does not feel understood or does not know where to draw the line. You might think, "Oh, my child knows there is a line they should not cross. We have discussed not hitting before, but it still happens." If that is true, they may not have another skill to replace it. If you want to remove troublesome behavior, you need a new skill to replace it.

A child can understand and maybe even get their way more frequently by replacing that hitting behavior with some skills. Educating a child not to hit is vital for building social, emotional, and academic skills.

Here are some steps to get started:

- If you want your child to understand that hitting hurts others and is not an acceptable way to resolve conflict, explain why hitting is wrong.
- Educate them about better ways of dealing with their frustrations and feelings, including talking about how they feel and finding a peaceful solution to their problems. Talk about soft touch.
- Clearly explain the rules and consequences for hitting to your children so they understand the consequences of their actions. It might be good to say, "We do not allow hitting in our house.

If you hurt someone, you must apologize and take some time out."

- Parental and other adult models of positive behavior play a significant role in children's development. Show others how to resolve conflicts peacefully by not hitting them.

- Children need to learn self-regulation techniques so they do not act out when angry or frustrated. Self-regulation techniques, such as breathing deeply or counting to ten, can help them calm down before reacting negatively.

- The best way to praise your child's positive behavior is when they successfully resolve a conflict without hitting. The use of positive reinforcement can help them learn to resolve conflicts more productively.

Imagine your child hitting another child who took their toy. You could say, "You should not hit others. You can use your words to tell them how you feel and ask for your toy back. If you hit again, you must apologize and take some time out." When the conflict arises, model positive behavior by showing them how to resolve it peacefully, such as asking, "I see you have my toy. Could I please have it back?" Finally, praise your child's positive behavior if they can resolve the conflict without hitting and reinforce that violence is not necessary to resolve conflicts.

To overcome hitting, a child also needs to be able to accept "No" answers and any boundaries they may have. For example, not eating a particular food or not touching a particular child are examples of boundaries not to be crossed.

The "No" Answer: How to Make Children Accept It

Teaching a child to accept a "No" can be challenging, but it is an essential lesson for building resilience, self-control, and emotional intelligence. A healthy way to teach children to accept a "No" is to follow the steps below:

1. When telling a child "No," explaining why is important. By doing this, they will be able to see that you are not just being arbitrary. For example, you could tell a child that you cannot buy a toy at the store because money is needed for groceries.

2. When saying "No" to a child, being firm and consistent is essential. Once you give in, they will learn that they will eventually get what they want if they push hard enough. In the future, they will have a harder time accepting a "No."

3. If you want to redirect your child's behavior, use positive language instead of saying "No" all the time. Rather than saying, "No, do not touch that," you could say, "Let us play with this toy instead."

4. You can offer your child an alternative if they have difficulty accepting a "No." For instance, if your child wants chocolate before dinner, you might say, "No, we cannot have chocolate now, but we can have it later."

5. If your child accepts a "No," emphasize their good behavior with positive reinforcement. In this situation, you might say, "You are a big winner for accepting a 'No' and finding something else to do."

Let us have a look at this example:

Suppose your child wants to watch a movie late at night on a school night. You could say, "No, we cannot watch a movie tonight because you need to get a good night's sleep as you have school tomorrow. Let us watch it on Friday when you will not have school the next day." By doing so, you explain to your child why you are saying "No" and then offer an alternative your child will accept. Whenever your child accepts your decision, reinforce their good behavior as much as possible.

Next, to stop children from hitting, you must assess and correct their behavior. For instance, when they communicate well, praise them for that. Similarly, if they fail to communicate well, ensure that you discuss this with them so they can participate in corrective teaching and earn a negative consequence. An attentive parent has the skills to correct their children calmly and is diligent about being watchful. If the child is consistently corrected for misbehavior, the child will be less likely to repeat that behavior.

Hitting hurts others and can negatively affect the hitter and the victim. We must aim to help our children develop the emotional and social skills they need to succeed by teaching them how to express their feelings and resolve conflicts peacefully and positively. The ultimate goal of teaching children not to hit is to build a peaceful, harmonious society where conflicts can be resolved without violence.

Chapter 17:
How to Discipline a Teenager Who Does Not Care About Consequences

Consequences are an important tool for teaching accountability and responsibility to children and teenagers. Consequences help children understand that their actions have outcomes and that they are responsible for those outcomes. When used effectively, consequences can help children learn to make better choices in the future. Good consequences are those that are appropriate for the behavior being addressed and are effective in changing that behavior. This consequence reinforces the broken rule and encourages the child to be accountable for their actions. Bad consequences are inappropriate or ineffective in addressing the behavior being addressed. This consequence does not effectively address the behavior and can lead to resentment and further lying. Practical consequences should be logical, age-appropriate, and enforceable. They should also be communicated clearly and consistently. For example, if a child hits another child, an appropriate consequence might be to have them take some time out and apologize to the other child. This consequence is logical because hitting hurts others, and it is age-appropriate because time out is effective for young children and enforceable since it can be implemented immediately. As a parent, people sometimes do some manipulative stuff, and the relationship becomes quite worse with their children.

Three factors make a good consequence:

- Keep it simple and predictable: Consequences do not need to be elaborate or ultra-creative to be effective. Sometimes I think parents do that for their benefit and that does not help the child. The more predictable and simpler a consequence is, the better.

- Relevance: The consequence needs to have some relevance for the child. That does not mean it needs to change every time. It cannot be something that you are doing just to hurt the child physically or mentally. Consequences do not have to hurt. That is one of the things that makes them so relevant.

- It should build character: The best consequence is one that builds character and leads the child to improve in some way. This is to get them to think about a problem and work out how to solve it so they will not have to deal with the same problem again. They must learn cause and effect. As long as a consequence teaches cause and effect in a predictable and relevant way, it will also help the child develop problem-solving skills.

Now, remember, bribing is not a good consequence. So, what do you do for positive consequences?

Sincere praises are what I call them. The type where you look into their eyes and tell them what they did was great. That positive consequence means something to the heart and gives them sincere, honest praise.

Another type of positive consequence is occasional motivators. We all get motivated by certain things. Make a list of what motivates your child. Does your teenager get motivated by free time? Do they get motivated by a little bit of game time? Doing stuff with friends? What is it that motivates them? Make a list and then occasionally pull out that list of motivators and use it to help them make plans for themselves as they are trying to conquer some of their troubling behaviors or get to the next level of doing something positive for themselves.

Teenagers value natural consequences, especially freedom-oriented things; the more trust you establish with someone, the more freedom they provide. So, you have to explain to them what you mean. They are more likely to be trusted by you if they follow instructions frequently, accept "No" answers, and help without asking. They will gain more freedom as a result.

Negative consequences can be an effective tool for teaching accountability and responsibility to teenagers. However, it is important to use them in limited numbers and ensure that they teach character and problem-solving skills. For example, house chores are one effective way to help teenagers learn to master themselves and accept the consequences calmly. Parents can empower teenagers to make better choices and learn from their mistakes by teaching them the value of hard work and responsibility.

It is also important for parents to focus on understanding their teenagers and empowering them rather than just disciplining them. Teenagers who feel like life has given up on them may need extra support and guidance to help them care about the consequences and take responsibility for their actions. By building a strong relationship with their teenagers, parents can help them learn to self-correct and make better choices in the future. Ultimately, the key principle for creating a successful home environment is self-government. Parents should bring their teenagers' attention to what needs to be corrected and teach them to accept the consequences calmly, building their problem-solving skills and confidence.

The following points can help us achieve that goal:

- There needs to be a certain tone and structure to create an environment where a person can learn how to self-correct and accept correction from others. The ideal tone is calmness. For instance, when giving feedback, the parent should avoid harsh language, name-calling, or criticism that would make the listener feel unvalued or disrespected.

- When you identify any problem with your teen, try to correct it. You need to accept that it happened. You must embrace the opportunity to teach or correct them and trust that the child wants to improve. For example, if your teen is caught shoplifting, do not ignore the problem or make excuses for them. Instead, sit down and have an open and honest conversation about why it happened and how to prevent it from happening again.

- Your home must be a place of understanding, trust, calmness, and acceptance.

- When you correct a child, you should let them use their disagreement skills. Parents should present negative consequences positively. For instance, instead of saying, "That was very naughty," you could say, "I do not like it when you do that, but I know you can do better."

- Discuss how you will correct your child. Also, discuss how they will deal with corrections. When your child knows how to handle corrections, they will stop power struggles with you. For example, you can let your child know that when they make a mistake, you will point it out and allow them to fix it independently.

Building trust with adolescents involves firm but fair discipline that encourages them to accept personal responsibility for their behavior. Teenagers can improve their decision-making and social and emotional development if their parents help them see the repercussions of their behavior. The goal of helping teenagers care about their consequences and become successful, responsible adults is not easy, but it can be accomplished with patience and consistency.

Chapter 18:
Parenting Tips for Disciplining an Oppositional Defiant Disorder

Parenting children with oppositional defiant disorder requires a strong foundation of trust and respect. Relationships between parents and children with ODD can be challenging due to children's struggle with authority figures. Nevertheless, parents can support their children's emotional and behavioral development by prioritizing trust and respect.

Keeping promises and commitments consistently is one way to build trust. The presence of a dependable adult in the life of a child with ODD may help them avoid feelings of mistrust or abandonment. Communicating honestly and transparently with their children is also a way for parents to build trust.

Effective parenting for children with ODD also encourages open communication and active listening. Children with ODD may have difficulty expressing or regulating their feelings, so creating a safe and supportive environment where they can share their thoughts and feelings is imperative. Listening to their children and validating their experiences can help parents encourage open communication. In addition, parents need to refrain from judging or criticizing their children and instead concentrate on understanding their viewpoints.

For children with ODD, establishing clear expectations and boundaries is crucial. As a result, it is essential to set clear guidelines for behavior and consequences for breaking these guidelines for children with ODD. By explaining to their child the consequences of breaking the rules and outlining their rules, parents can establish clear expectations. Furthermore, these consequences and expectations should be enforced consistently. This way, children with ODD will feel secure and know what to expect.

Children with this disorder require effective discipline strategies to manage their symptoms and develop positive behavioral habits. There are several effective discipline approaches you can use depending on the child's individual needs and symptoms:

- Positive reinforcement aims to encourage positive behaviors through rewards and praise. This reinforcement may encourage children with ODD to continue positive behavior and increase their self-esteem. If a child completes a task or exhibits positive behavior, parents should reward them with extra screen time or a special treat. Praise and recognition can also motivate children with ODD.

- Children with ODD need clear consequences for negative behavior and consistent reinforcement of those consequences. Setting clear guidelines for behavior and enforcing consequences for breaking these guidelines is a good idea for parents. To help children with ODD understand why rules and boundaries are important, they should consistently enforce these rules and consequences. The approach can help children with ODD feel secure and understand what is expected of them.

- A time out can be an effective punishment for disruptive or aggressive behavior. Parents can designate a space in their home where their children can calm down and reflect on their behavior. Time out spaces should be safe and distraction-free. Parents, along with the expected duration, should also explain time outs. An approach like this can help children with ODD learn to regulate their emotions and self-regulate.

- Parents may overlook minor misbehaviors to avoid power struggles to focus on more significant issues. Negative attention-seeking behavior can also be prevented by ignoring minor misbehaviors. Despite this, parents should ensure they do not enable negative behaviors by ignoring them.

- Children with ODD can benefit from collaborative problem-solving when they are involved in identifying solutions to behavioral challenges. A collaborative approach to problem-solving involves sitting down with the child and identifying the underlying cause of their behavior. Developing problem-solving skills and feeling empowered can help children with the disorder better manage their behavior with this approach.

Parents dealing with a child with oppositional defiant disorder often find it difficult to manage the disorder independently. Children with ODD require support from mental health professionals. Parents should consider the following factors:

- Parents must seek professional help for children with ODD as soon as possible. A mental health professional can tailor the diagnosis and treatment plan to meet the child's needs. Early intervention can also prevent more severe emotional and behavioral problems in the future.

- Working with mental health professionals effectively establishes a comprehensive treatment plan focusing on the child's emotional, behavioral, and social needs. The child's symptoms can be managed through counseling, behavioral therapy, and other interventions provided by mental health professionals. The therapists can also work with parents to develop strategies supporting the child's treatment plan.

- Children with ODD may benefit from medication to manage their symptoms. Medication that treats symptoms such as impulsivity, hyperactivity, and irritability, such as stimulants or antidepressants, can be helpful. A comprehensive treatment program, however, should combine medication with other interventions like counseling and therapy.

- A mental health professional's role includes dealing with the child's symptoms and supporting their family. It is common for parents to feel overwhelmed or stressed by their children's behavior, and they may benefit from counseling or support groups. Parenting a child with ODD can be challenging, but mental health professionals can provide resources and support. A critical aspect of supporting children with ODD is the involvement of mental health professionals. A detailed treatment plan should be developed with mental health professionals, and parents should understand how medication can help manage symptoms of ODD. Mental health professionals can also provide support and resources to help parents manage the emotional and behavioral challenges of raising a child with ODD.

In short, when parenting a child with an oppositional defiant disorder, parents can use effective strategies to help their child develop emotionally and behaviorally. A strong foundation of trust and respect is key to disciplining a child with ODD. Aside from encouraging open communication, they also encourage active listening. Working collaboratively to solve behavioral problems, the team establishes clear expectations and boundaries, reinforces positive behavior, and enforces consistent consequences. Discipline strategies should be tailored to the child's individual needs and symptoms. Mental health professionals should be consulted to develop a comprehensive treatment plan for children. Parents should be involved in developing these strategies and be educated on how to implement them. Regular treatment plan reviews should be conducted to ensure it is effective and working for the child.

Chapter 19:
25 Privileges Children Can Earn for Following the Rules and Having "Good Behavior"

An effective method for developing and reinforcing beneficial habits in youngsters is to reward them. Rewarding positive behavior in children has many benefits, including encouraging further appropriate behavior, increasing the child's sense of self-worth and confidence, and strengthening the bond between the child and the adult providing the reward. It is crucial to remember that not all incentives are the same. Meaningful, diversified, and in line with family values are all qualities of effective incentives. Negative incentives, on the other hand, are those that are ineffective, harmful, inconsistent, or promote materialism. Parents and caregivers must pick rewards wisely to encourage constructive behaviors and discourage harmful ones.

Here are some suggestions for suitable rewards, but you can add your own:

1. Extra screen time: Children who follow the rules and behave well can earn extra screen time, like watching TV or playing video games for an additional half-hour.

2. Later bedtime: Children who behave well can earn a later bedtime on weekends, such as staying up an additional 30 minutes.

3. Choose dinner: Children can choose what they want for dinner on a particular evening.

4. Get a treat: Children can earn a special treat such as ice cream or a small toy.

5. Choose a family activity: Children can earn the privilege of choosing a fun family activity, such as walking to the park or playing a board game.

6. Have a sleepover: Children can earn the privilege of having a friend stay over for a night.

7. Pick the movie: Children can choose a family movie for movie night.

8. Extra dessert: Children can earn an extra dessert or sweet treat after dinner.

9. Have a picnic: Children can earn the privilege of picnicking with the family on a nice day.

10. Taking kids to a museum or theme park: Children can earn the privilege of visiting a museum or other educational activity.

11. Make a special arts and crafts activity: Do a special arts and crafts activity such as making socks or paper bag puppets, or paper plate masks.

12. Have a party: Children can earn a small party with friends or family.

13. Earning an allowance or extra pocket money: By giving children a clear reward for good behavior, they will be more likely to make good decisions and understand the consequences.

14. Get a new book: Children can choose their favorite book or magazine to read.

15. Choose a new game: Children can choose a new board or video game.

16. Go out for ice cream: Children can earn going out for ice cream or frozen yogurt.

17. Play a sport: Children can earn the privilege of playing a sport or activity of their choice.
18. Choose the weekend breakfast menu: Giving children the opportunity to choose the weekend breakfast menu reinforces the notion that choices matter and rewards can be earned.
19. Taking kids to the movies: Children can earn the privilege of watching movies with family or friends.
20. Choose a restaurant: Children can choose a restaurant for dinner.
21. Have a "staycation": Children can earn the privilege of having a fun stay-at-home vacation, such as setting up a backyard campsite or having a spa day.
22. Pick a family pet or its name: A reward like this encourages children to follow good behavior and teaches them responsibility. Also, it helps them learn the value of making good decisions.
23. Have a "no chores" day: Children can earn a day without chores or responsibilities.
24. Get a gift card: Gift cards to favorite stores and restaurants can be given to children as a reward.
25. Choose the family holiday decoration: To earn the privilege to choose the family's holiday decorations or traditions, a child must demonstrate a level of responsibility and good behavior that the family values.

The privileges do not need to be extravagant or expensive. They can be as simple as choosing stickers or taking pictures of themselves.

When to Reward a Child

- Once they have finished one task (homework, chore, etc.).

- When completing multiple tasks in a row (completing homework, cleaning up after dinner, putting on pajamas, brushing teeth).

- Following rules for a certain period, such as an hour, a day, or a week.

- A weekend privilege can be earned by your child at the end of a successful week (such as completing their homework every night).

- When you have had a good day or week at school (you have not received any negative phone calls from the teacher or principal).

It is important to avoid withholding rewards as punishment, as this can lead to confusion and frustration for the child. Additionally, rewards should not be given for expected behaviors or are part of the child's normal routine. Instead, rewards should be given for behaviors above and beyond what is expected, such as helping others, showing kindness, or exhibiting self-control in a challenging situation. Parents and caregivers should use discretion to determine when and how often to reward their children based on their needs and behavior patterns.

Children's good behavior can be encouraged and reinforced using rewards. Children's self-esteem, connection with their caregivers, and willingness to follow the rules can all benefit from well-implemented reward systems. Meaningful, diversified, and in line with family values are all qualities of successful incentives. Rewards are used to encourage desirable behaviors, not to replace discipline. Parents and teachers can aid their children in the development of responsibility, self-control, and respect for others by using rewards for appropriate behavior. Rewards encourage lifelong positive behavior patterns in children.

Chapter 20:
Discipline Tips for Kids With Oppositional Defiant Disorder

Oppositional defiant disorder can be challenging for children and their parents. ODD is characterized by persistent angry and defiant behavior. Common symptoms include losing temper, arguing with adults, and deliberately defying rules. Treatment options include cognitive-behavioral therapy, parent training, and, in extreme cases, medication. Here are a few discipline tips to help parents manage their child's behavior and improve their family's quality of life. Being the parent of an ODD child can be exhausting, overwhelming, and discouraging, but let me tell you there is hope. It is important to remember that children with ODD can and do make progress. With the right tools, parents can learn to manage behavior effectively and create a supportive and positive environment for their children. Parents can help their children with ODD reach their full potential with patience, understanding, and support.

Some discipline tips include:

- You should set clear and consistent rules for your child's behavior and enforce them consistently. Your kid will feel safer and more in charge of their own life when they know what is expected. Remember your rules and do not argue, lecture, or make sarcastic remarks about your child. Consider your rules and their appropriateness for your child, and state them accordingly. You should not force them to do anything; instead, encourage and remind them that good behavior will be rewarded. Keep your voice calm and logical. Consistently and without emotion enforce the consequences of breaking a rule. Children will learn to take responsibility for their actions by understanding the consequences of their actions. When you follow a rule and mean it, your child will learn to respect and take your words seriously. Children with ODD can be challenging to discipline, and it may take time and patience to see improvement. Do not give up or lose hope; continue working with your child to develop positive habits.

- Try to anticipate situations that may trigger your child's negative behavior and take steps to prevent them from occurring. For example, if your child has difficulty with transitions, give them plenty of warning before switching activities.

- When your kid feels overwhelmed or irritated, a time out may be an excellent approach to help them take a break and calm down. Make sure to use them consistently and calmly. You can help your ODD child by remaining calm and using meditation and deep breathing techniques. You can also try teaching them grounding techniques to reduce anxiety for them and you.

- Stay calm when they are in a rage or their behavior is not good. Hug them to help them feel calm and safe and to reinforce that everything is okay and that you love them unconditionally.

- Give them a choice. Calm down, stay logical, and explain that they can choose A or B to feel they have some control. Giving your child choices can help them feel more in control and reduce the likelihood of a power struggle. Research indicates that giving children choices improves behavior.

- Children learn by example, so model good behavior and positive coping skills. This can help your child learn to manage their emotions and behavior healthily.

- Parenting a child with ODD can be challenging, and seeking support from family, friends, or a mental health professional is important. This can help you manage stress and develop effective discipline strategies.

- Taking care of yourself is essential when parenting a child with ODD. Make sure to prioritize self-care activities such as exercise, time with friends, or relaxation techniques to help you stay grounded and focused.

- Set up expectations ahead of time and enforce them with boundaries. This is much more effective than punishing your child or taking away privileges.

- Give your kid a say in what they want to do. Instead of threatening to take anything away if they do not behave, remind them of what they are working for.

- Try using transition warnings to help your youngster prepare for what is to come. Children who do not have a sense of time may benefit from using a timer or visual timer.

- Treatment strategies for a child with ODD or related symptoms include showing them you understand how they feel and allowing them to have some time on the computer again tomorrow.

- The term "can" should be eliminated from directive language if feasible. If possible, offer them something else to do or point them toward something they might enjoy.

- When your child follows your expectations or listens to your directions, reinforce those behaviors with specific praise. Positive rewards can include praise, stickers, and other rewards for good behavior. The result can be an increase in your child's confidence and positive behavior.

- If possible, create a schedule with your child that includes chores, homework, self-help tasks, and fun activities. Mini schedules are a shortened variation of a typical schedule that can include as few as two or three steps.

- When your child is acting badly, try to look at things from a logical aspect rather than an emotional aspect, and try to take excess emotion out unless it is positive for good behavior.

- Children with ODD often have poor self-esteem and loathe themselves because they do not get positive feedback or affection. Try to be kind and affectionate, and spend some one-on-one time with them doing something fun they enjoy.

- If your kids are not well-rested, well-hydrated, or eating something nourishing on a somewhat regular basis, they will feel worse and act worse. Encourage them to eat healthy foods, drink plenty of water, and get to bed quickly.

Parents of kids with oppositional defiant disorder may find it challenging and exhausting. You can, however, help your child achieve greater harmony and support by following the tips listed above. Provide your child with opportunities to exercise control and make choices. Set clear and consistent boundaries, use positive reinforcement, and seek professional help when necessary. Parenting your child can be a rewarding experience if you are patient, understanding, and willing to adapt your style.

Part 3:
Building Positive Relationships and Communication

Chapter 21:
Stop Yelling at Your Kids

Yelling at children can negatively impact both the parent and the child, so it is crucial to avoid it. Yelling can lead to a breakdown in the relationship between the parent and the child, causing the child to feel anxious, scared, and unloved. It can also negatively affect them emotionally, leading to feelings of powerlessness, humiliation, and rejection. Furthermore, yelling is not a viable method of disciplining a child because it does not teach them how to behave differently in the future and can make them more resistant to change. Stress levels of the child and parent can increase due to yelling, which negatively impacts their mental and physical health. To create a healthy and positive environment for the child and parent, avoiding yelling and using effective discipline methods is important.

Here are a few ways parents can use to avoid yelling at their children:

- As parents, practicing mindfulness to recognize our thoughts and emotions is imperative. Taking deep breaths or meditating can help us stay calm when emotions escalate. To practice mindfulness, we need to be present in the moment and observe our thoughts and feelings without judgment. We can focus on breathing or a mantra to stay present and mindful. For example, we can take three deep breaths and count to ten before responding to a situation that makes us angry. We can also practice mindfulness by being aware of our bodies and noticing any tension or tightness. Taking a few moments to exercise mindfulness can help us stay calm and centered in difficult moments.

- Developing alternative responses is helpful when our child behaves in a way that upsets us. We can use positive reinforcement, praise, or redirection to steer our child's behavior in a positive direction. For instance, rather than scolding a child for not completing their homework, we can suggest they take a break and return to the task with a fresh perspective. This approach helps teach our children healthy coping skills, encourages them to take responsibility for their actions, and builds their self-esteem. It also allows us to model good behavior and teach our children how to handle negative emotions constructively.

- Breaks are crucial when we feel overwhelmed. We can walk or take a few minutes to calm down. For example, if we feel overwhelmed by our child's misbehavior, we could step away for a few moments and inhale/exhale several deep breaths. This will help us remain calm and collected. Taking a break allows us to step back, take a few moments to review the situation, and devise the best course of action. It also allows us to reset our mindset and refocus more positively.

- Sometimes, seeking support from family, friends, or counselors can help us develop new insights and perspectives. Family and friends can offer emotional support, while counselors can provide more objective advice and insights. Having someone to talk to can help us gain clarity and understanding of our thoughts and feelings. Through conversation, we can gain insight into why we might feel a certain way or have difficulty dealing with a situation.

- Establishing clear boundaries and consequences for our child's behavior can reduce parental frustration and create a more peaceful environment at home. For instance, we might agree to a rule that states that if our child does not complete their homework by 8 p.m., they will not be able to watch TV the following day. In addition, if our child breaks a rule, we can set a consequence such as no playing with friends for the following day.

- As parents, we should model positive behavior for our children. Children often mimic our behavior, so if they see us reacting calmly and positively to difficult situations, they are more likely to do the same. For instance, when faced with a stressful situation, like getting stuck in traffic, instead of yelling and becoming angry, we can take deep breaths and explain to our children that it is normal to feel frustrated and that we can use the time to talk and get to know each other better.

- Using "I" statements instead of "you" when communicating with our child can be more effective and less confrontational. For example, saying, "I feel frustrated when you do not listen to me," instead of "You never listen to me," can be more effective. By using "I" instead of "you" in statements, we can show our child that we are looking for a resolution rather than a confrontation, thereby strengthening our relationship.

- Identifying our anger and yelling triggers, such as lack of sleep, stress at work, or certain behaviors from our child, can help us avoid or manage them. For instance, if we know that we are more likely to yell when we are tired, we can try to get more sleep or take a break when we start to feel our frustration levels rising.

- When communicating with our child, active listening means listening without interrupting, judging, or reacting emotionally. This can help us understand our child's perspective and respond more effectively. For instance, when a child is upset about something, actively listening can help us understand why they feel this way and offer appropriate comfort and guidance.

- Implementing a "calm down" routine when our emotions escalate can help us stay calm and respond to our child positively. This can be as simple as taking a deep breath or finding something to focus on, like a relaxing scene or an object in the room. Additionally, adding calming exercises or activities into our routine can help us manage our emotions better. This could include walking, journaling our thoughts, or engaging in a mindful activity. Taking a few moments to practice calming activities can help us better manage our emotions and be better prepared to respond to our children positively.

When you stop yelling as a parent, you can reap various benefits. Establishing an environment of trust, respect, and love can improve your relationship with your child. Positive reinforcement and effective discipline techniques can help parents teach their children better behavior and encourage positive long-term changes. A calmer and healthier household can be achieved by reducing yelling for parents and children. Additionally, effective discipline techniques can lead to greater parental satisfaction and fulfillment, increasing confidence in the parent's parenting abilities. It is possible to make your family life more fulfilling, healthier, and happier by stopping yelling.

Chapter 22:
Best Exercises and Activities for Oppositional Defiant Disorder

Raising children with oppositional defiant disorder can be hard and tiring. Children with ODD can be argumentative, defiant, and resistant to authority. This can make it hard to build and keep healthy relationships with them. But some exercises and activities can help kids with this disorder control their behavior and feel better overall. This chapter aims to look at some of the best exercises and activities that parents and other caretakers can do with their ODD child to help them. With exercise and mindfulness practices, your child can learn important life skills, reduce stress, and better control their behavior.

- Art therapy helps kids express themselves creatively and express their feelings safely and in a controlled way. Art therapy gives kids a way to express their feelings and emotions without having to use words. It also gives them a safe place to discuss hard things without fear. This can help them feel better about themselves, sort out their thoughts, and learn how to solve problems better.

- Outdoor sports like soccer, basketball, and other team sports can teach kids to work together, communicate, and be good sports. Children's physical and mental health can benefit from playing sports outside.

- Drama or acting classes can help kids learn to communicate well, express themselves, and feel more confident. Through drama and acting classes, kids can try out different roles and feelings, which can help them learn more about themselves and others. It also allows kids to collaborate and develop their creative skills.

- By doing yoga or mindfulness meditation, kids can learn to control their feelings and deal with stress. Children can feel and talk about a wide range of emotions in a safe space by doing things like improvising. This helps them learn how to deal with their feelings, which can help them in their everyday lives.

- Kids can learn self-discipline and self-control through karate, judo, and taekwondo. Martial arts help kids learn to concentrate and set and reach their goals. When done regularly, these activities can help build emotional intelligence and resilience, which will be useful in the long run.

- Music therapy helps kids work through their feelings, which can help them become emotionally smart and strong.

- Dance classes can help kids improve their coordination, balance, and awareness of their bodies. Dance classes can also help people feel more confident and give them a sense of accomplishment. Dance can also help kids learn to get along with others, follow directions, and work as a team.

- When kids spend time with animals, like therapy dogs or horses, they can learn to trust and care about others. Animal-assisted therapy helps kids connect with animals in a safe, caring setting, which can be comforting and loving. It can also reduce stress and help people get along better with each other.

- Gardening teaches kids to be patient, care for others, and be responsible. Children learn how to care for a living thing, and seeing the results of their work makes them feel good. It also helps them feel better about themselves and better understand the world around them.

- Cooking or baking can help kids learn to follow directions, be patient, and eat well. By cooking or baking, they learn to make something from scratch and feel proud of what they have made. This can help them feel good about themselves and feel more confident.

- Children can learn empathy, compassion, and purpose by volunteering for a charity or community group. It also shows them how important it is to work as a team and give back to the community. Volunteering can allow them to put their skills and talents to good use and make them feel like they belong and are connected.

- Reading or writing can help kids improve at talking to people and thinking of more ideas. Children can improve their language and communication skills by reading and writing, which also helps them learn more about the world around them.

- Children can learn to follow the rules, take turns, and solve problems by playing board games. Children can also learn how to get along with other people, make friends, and work as a team by playing board games.

- Science experiments can help kids learn to watch, ask questions, and try things out. Science experiments allow children to learn more about the scientific method and how things work. It can also help them learn how to think critically and solve problems as they try to find answers to the problems they are given.

- Building with blocks, Legos, or other items can help kids learn about space, be creative, and figure out how to solve problems. These activities teach kids how to think about things more broadly, how to picture their ideas, and how to put those ideas into action. It also helps them feel good about themselves and their ability to make something real.

- Swimming and other water activities can help kids get better at coordination, strength, and stamina. Children can learn how to use different body movements to get what they want by swimming or doing other water activities. For example, they can learn how to move their arms and legs to swim faster or further. This teaches them to think about how their bodies move and how they can use those movements to reach their goals. Visualizing their ideas and putting them to use, like in a swimming race, also gives them more confidence in their skills.

- Children can connect with nature by spending time outside. They develop a sense of awe and wonder. This not only helps kids learn to be creative and think outside the box, but it also helps them improve their large motor skills, spatial awareness, and hand-eye coordination. Children on regular nature walk feel a stronger connection to their bodies and the natural environment. This can help them develop a sense of respect and appreciation for the natural world.

- Photography and videography are fun ways for kids to show their creativity and learn how to communicate visually. Children are taught to pay attention to their surroundings and creatively record them through activities like photography and videography. This lets them know their surroundings and learn how their actions can change the world around them.

- Writing in a journal can help kids work through their feelings and learn more about themselves. Through these activities and writing in a journal, kids can learn to care about their surroundings, understand how things work, and talk about how they feel safely and creatively. This can help them become more resilient and connect to their world.

- Kids can learn to get along with people and make new friends by participating in a program to improve their social skills. Through these groups, kids can work on their social skills in a safe, supportive setting and get feedback from their peers and the person in charge of the group. This helps them learn how to read social cues and know what to do in different situations.

Children with oppositional defiant disorder can benefit from several exercises and activities. Physical activity, like sports or yoga, can help relieve stress and make them feel better overall. Mindfulness activities, like breathing exercises and meditation, can help kids learn to control their feelings and act better. Moreover, social activities and hobbies like music or art classes can be a healthy way to express themselves and teaches them how to get along with others. In the end, finding the right exercises and activities for your child with ODD may take some trial and error. But if you give your child various ways to explore their interests and learn important life skills, you can help them become more optimistic about life and improve their overall health.

Chapter 23:
The Importance of Building Self-Esteem

Children's development and future happiness depend on their ability to develop a healthy sense of self-worth. Children with a strong sense of self-worth have an optimistic attitude, can bounce back from disappointments, and are prepared to face and overcome obstacles. Confident and capable youngsters are more inclined to take risks, use their voices, and form strong bonds with those around them. Furthermore, youngsters with a solid sense of self-worth are better equipped to deal with school and workplace stresses. As children's self-esteem may significantly impact their growth and development, fostering and nourishing it early is crucial. Children's self-esteem can be fostered when adults around them are encouraging, positive role models, providing ample opportunity for growth and development.

Importance of Good Self-Esteem for a Child

Self-esteem is crucial to the well-being and success of a child. Good self-esteem leads to a positive outlook on life, a sense of confidence in one's abilities, and greater resilience to stress and difficulties. Self-esteem is linked to better academic performance, positive relationships, and self-image. It is also linked to a lower anxiety and depression rate. By giving love and support, offering opportunities for exploration and learning, and celebrating children's achievements and strengths, parents, caregivers, and educators can help children develop good self-esteem. So, children can become confident, resilient, and successful adults, equipped with the tools to handle challenges and obstacles and thrive in all aspects of their lives as adults.

How Positive Self-Esteem Develops

The development of positive self-esteem involves both internal and external factors. To develop positive self-esteem, a child must consider internal factors, such as temperament and personality, and external factors, such as experiences, relationships, and cultural influences. Successful children receive praise or feel success can boost their self-esteem and feel good about their abilities after completing a task. The love and validation children receive from parents, caregivers, and other important adults can help them develop a positive view of themselves. Self-esteem is also improved through positive self-talk and feeling competent. Cultural values and beliefs can also influence self-worth. It is more likely that children will have positive self-esteem when they grow up in a culture that values individualism, autonomy, and self-expression. The best way to help children develop positive self-esteem is to provide love and support, opportunities for exploration and learning, celebrate their strengths and achievements, and model positive attitudes and behaviors. Developing a positive sense of self-esteem in children will ensure confidence, resilience, and success as they navigate through life.

What Can Parents Do to Boost Their Children's Self-Esteem?

The role of parents in boosting the self-esteem of their children is crucial. To help their child develop a healthy sense of self-worth, parents can implement the following strategies:

- Children develop a positive self-image when they feel loved and supported. Parents need to show affection, spend quality time with their children, and be attentive and present to provide love and support to their children. When children feel loved, supported, and valued, they better appreciate who they are and what they can accomplish. This can also give them the courage to take risks and try new things, which helps them gain self-confidence and a positive self-image.

- Do not just praise achievements, praise efforts. Parents can praise their children's efforts and hard work rather than their achievements. Success is more about effort and perseverance than innate abilities, which helps children understand the value of hard work and perseverance. This helps children develop a growth mindset and learn to accept failure as part of the learning process. Giving children positive feedback on their effort can also help boost their confidence and motivation.

- Provide opportunities for children to make their own decisions and choices. Parents can encourage their children's independence by providing them with opportunities. As a result, children feel capable and confident about their abilities. This also helps children develop problem-solving skills, as they must think through their options and analyze the consequences of their decisions. Moreover, it teaches them the importance of responsibility and respect for the decisions of others.

- Children can be given challenges appropriate to their age and abilities when their parents offer them. In this way, children develop skills and confidence as they overcome challenges. This allows them to expand their horizons and become more resilient. It also helps them to understand the importance of setting realistic goals and working hard to reach them. Supporting children in this way can have a lasting impact on their lives.

- The best way to model positive self-talk is to speak positively about yourself and your abilities. Children gain self-confidence and self-esteem by speaking positively about themselves. Modeling positive self-talk for children can help them develop a more positive outlook on their abilities and recognize their worth. This can also lead to improved academic performance, healthier relationships, and increased resilience.

- A child's self-esteem can be damaged by harsh criticism or negative feedback from parents. Feedback and encouragement should instead be offered constructively. When children receive criticism or negative feedback, they often internalize it and view themselves as failures. On the other hand, when parents provide feedback and encouragement constructively, children can learn from their mistakes and gain confidence in their abilities.

- Every child should be celebrated for their strengths and accomplishments, big or small. A sense of value and appreciation for a child's individuality can be fostered in this way. This is important because when children feel valued and appreciated, their self-esteem increases. They are more likely to be confident in their abilities and feel motivated to achieve their goals.

Be an example of what you want to see in others. Setting a good example begins with what you do daily (raking leaves, making a meal, cleaning dishes, or washing your car). As your child does homework, cleans up toys, or makes the bed, they learn to put effort into them. Attitude matters. Your child learns to do the same thing when you do things cheerfully (or at least without grumbling or complaining). You can teach your child to take pride in a well-done job by taking your time and not rushing through chores.

Chapter 24:
Self-Esteem Journal

A self-esteem journal is a type of journal or diary used to help individuals develop and maintain a positive sense of self-worth. It is a tool for self-reflection, self-discovery, and self-improvement, allowing individuals to track their progress toward healthy self-esteem.

In a self-esteem journal, individuals can record their thoughts, feelings, and experiences related to their self-esteem. They can identify their strengths and weaknesses, set self-improvement goals, and track their progress. Additionally, individuals can use their self-esteem journal to challenge negative self-talk and switch it with positive affirmations.

A self-esteem journal can take many forms, including a traditional paper journal, a digital journal, or an app. Some journals provide prompts or exercises to help individuals explore and develop their self-esteem, while others allow individuals to customize their prompts and exercises.

How Does a Self-Esteem Journal Help?

Self-esteem journaling is valuable for developing and maintaining a positive sense of self-worth. Some of the most important gains from keeping a self-esteem diary are:

- Self-reflection: Self-esteem journaling allows individuals to reflect on their thoughts, feelings, and experiences related to their self-esteem. This can help them identify negative self-talk patterns, challenge limiting beliefs, and develop a more positive and realistic self-image.

- Goal setting: Self-esteem journaling can help individuals set self-improvement goals and track their progress toward them. This can help individuals feel more in control of their lives and confident in their abilities.

- Accountability: Self-esteem journaling can help individuals hold themselves accountable for their actions and choices. By tracking their progress toward self-improvement goals, individuals can stay motivated and focused on their goals.

- Stress reduction: Journaling has been shown to reduce stress and improve mental health outcomes. Individuals can reduce anxiety and improve their well-being by reflecting on their thoughts and feelings in a safe and non-judgmental space.

- Positive self-talk: Self-esteem journaling can help individuals replace negative self-talk with positive affirmations. A more positive and accurate perception of oneself can be developed by examining one's qualities and successes.

How Do You Write a Self-Esteem Journal?

What to write in a self-esteem journal depends on the individual's specific goals and needs. However, here are some general prompts to help individuals get started with self-esteem journaling:

- Write down your strengths and accomplishments: This can help you focus on your positive qualities and build a positive self-image.

- Identify negative self-talk patterns and challenge them: Write down any negative thoughts or beliefs about yourself and challenge them with evidence to the contrary.

- Set self-improvement goals: Write down specific goals for yourself and the steps you plan to take to achieve them.

- Reflect on your positive experiences: Write down any positive experiences you have had, including compliments or accomplishments you have achieved.

- Practice gratitude: Write down things you are grateful for, including positive relationships, experiences, or qualities about yourself.

- Write down your affirmations.: Affirmations are phrases that may be repeated to oneself regularly to change negative thought patterns and encourage positive thinking, self-esteem, and motivation.

How Do I Convince My Child to Keep a Self-Esteem Journal?

Encouraging your child to keep a self-esteem journal can effectively support their emotional well-being and foster a more positive self-perception. Let them write down affirmations that are meaningful and relevant to them.

They should reflect on their personal growth. They should write down any ways they have grown or changed over time, including new skills they have developed or challenges they have overcome.

Here are some tips for persuading your child to keep a self-esteem journal:

- Explain the benefits: Talk to your child about the benefits of keeping a self-esteem journal, such as building self-confidence, reducing stress, and improving mental health. Help them understand how this practice can benefit them and their overall well-being.

- Make it fun: Encourage your child to decorate their journal with stickers, markers, or other art supplies to enhance it to be more appealing and personal to them. Let them choose a journal they like and encourage them to personalize it to make it their own.

- Set a regular time: Help your child establish a regular time to write in their journal, such as before bedtime or in the morning. Encourage them to make it a part of their daily routine and offer gentle reminders to stay on track.

- Provide prompts: If your child struggles to develop things to write about, give them prompts or questions to get them started. Ask them to reflect on positive experiences, identify their strengths, or set goals for self-improvement.

- Lead by example: Show your child that you value self-reflection and personal growth by keeping a journal. Let them see what you write in your journal, and talk to them about how it helps you.

- Celebrate progress: Encourage your child to celebrate their progress and successes, no matter how small, acknowledge their hard work and success, and highlight their many redeeming traits.

Self-esteem journals help individuals develop and maintain a positive sense of self-worth. Writing in a journal regularly and being honest about thoughts and feelings can help build a healthier self-esteem and a more optimistic outlook. By reflecting on one's thoughts and experiences, identifying negative self-talk patterns, setting self-improvement goals, and practicing gratitude and affirmations, individuals can cultivate a more positive self-image and build resilience against negative self-judgment. A self-esteem journal can also serve as a tool for accountability and motivation toward achieving self-improvement goals, reducing stress, and improving overall mental health. Regular self-esteem journaling can be a powerful practice for individuals seeking to improve their self-esteem and live a more fulfilling life.

Let me end this chapter with the true story of a strong mother.

The narrator is a single mother with an 11-year-old child with an oppositional defiant disorder, attention deficit hyperactivity disorder, and anxiety. She has noticed that her child's self-esteem has suffered due to various challenges, including meltdowns, feeling different from his friends, and being bullied at daycare. The narrator started a self-esteem journal to help her child develop a more positive self-image. Every night before bed, they discuss two things the child is proud of from the day. The writer fills the rest of the page with things she is proud of. The child does not like writing, so the writer does it. Over time, the nightly ritual helped the child think higher about himself. Although the process has changed over the years, it has remained a positive experience for both the mother and her child. The narrator believes that the self-esteem journal has helped build a foundation of trust and positivity to help them navigate puberty and the teenage years.

Chapter 25:
Get More Cooperation

You might find navigating family and social relationships challenging when parenting an oppositional defiant disorder child.

In that case, consider the following methods:

- Educate about ODD.
- Be specific about your needs.
- Set boundaries.
- Encourage positive interactions.
- Offer guidance about practicing empathy.
- Take care of yourself.

Parenting a child with ODD requires a support system. You and your child can thrive when you educate family and friends, set boundaries, encourage positive interactions, offer guidance, and take care of yourself.

- **Educate About ODD**

Parents of children diagnosed with oppositional defiant disorder are responsible for informing their social networks about their child's condition, its symptoms, and its impact on the family. This allows them to understand you and your child. If your child exhibits specific symptoms such as tantrums, argumentative behavior, or stubbornness, you can provide them with information about those symptoms. Furthermore, you can explain how these symptoms can affect your child's daily life, such as difficulties in school, peer relationships, and family stress. Providing family and friends with resources and information can make them feel better prepared to support you and your child. Books, articles, and online resources can provide insight into how to interact with children with ODD. Discuss strategies that can help children with ODD in their difficult times.

- **Be Specific About Your Needs**

If you are parenting a child with an oppositional defiant disorder, you need to communicate your needs clearly and specifically to your family and friends. Let them know what kind of support you need (childcare, housework, or emotional support).

When you are specific about what you and your child need, friends and family can better support you. You might be able to ask your family and friends to watch your child for a few hours a week if you need help with childcare. Cooking, cleaning, or running errands can all be done with the help of someone willing to assist you with household chores. You can seek emotional support from someone to voice your concerns or stay positive when faced with challenges.

Clear and direct communication is important when communicating your needs. Be sure to inform your family and friends of your needs and how they can assist. Ask for help when needed, and be honest about your limitations. When you are stressed or overwhelmed, this is especially important.

Family and friends may not always know what kind of support you need, so it is OK to ask for help or provide guidance on how they can best help you and your child. If you are specific about your needs, you can create an environment that supports you and your child.

- **Set Boundaries**

Setting clear boundaries with family and friends is important when parenting a child with ODD. To maintain a supportive environment for your child, you should let them know what you are and are unwilling to tolerate.

For example, you may also have rules regarding how family and friends can interact with the child, such as not shouting or speaking calmly. Enforcing these boundaries consistently is important. Communicating your boundaries clearly and directly is crucial. Your child's well-being depends on describing what is and is not acceptable behavior to family and friends. Keep your boundaries firm, but be willing to negotiate and compromise when necessary.

- **Encourage Positive Interactions**

To parent a child with ODD, you must encourage family and friends to interact positively with your child, even if it is just a simple greeting. Building your child's self-esteem and improving their behavior can be achieved through positive interactions. For example, you can ask family and friends to be interested in your child's hobbies, to praise them for their achievements, or to say hello. Positive interactions can also influence your child's attitudes and behaviors. You can remind your child that they are loved and valued through positive interactions with family members and friends if your child behaves negatively or disrespectfully. You may need to assist family and friends in positively interacting with your child. Be patient and understanding.

- **Offer Guidance About Practicing Empathy**

Empathy is an important strategy for getting family and friends to cooperate with a child with ODD. Understanding your child's perspective and feelings, validating their emotions, and showing that you understand why they may be frustrated or upset are all aspects of empathy. You can also communicate constructively and respectfully with family and friends about your child's behavior by practicing empathy. Empathy allows you to approach the situation with understanding and compassion instead of blaming or criticizing your child. Clarify to family and friends why your child may struggle by explaining how certain situations or behaviors can trigger negative reactions. Creating a compassionate and supportive environment for your child to thrive can be accomplished by acknowledging their feelings and helping others understand their perspective.

- **Take Care of Yourself**

To get family and friends' cooperation when parenting an oppositional defiant disorder child, it is very important to take care of yourself. In addition to improving your emotional well-being, prioritizing your own needs can help you better manage stress, communicate with your child, and interact with others. You can take care of yourself in various ways, including ensuring that you get enough sleep, exercise, and provide emotional support. Spare time for your favorite activities, such as reading books, listening to music, or spending time with friends, can help you achieve this goal. It's also important to seek professional help when needed. Depending on your situation, you may need therapy or counseling for yourself, your child, or your entire family. Developing coping strategies, improving communication skills, and learning new approaches to managing your child's behavior can be learned from a mental health professional. Do not hesitate to ask for help; let them know if you need it.

Although parenting a kid with ODD might be difficult, it is possible to establish a positive atmosphere for both you and your child with the appropriate approach. Educating family and friends about ODD, being specific about your needs, setting clear boundaries, encouraging positive interactions, practicing empathy, and taking care of yourself can all help you get cooperation from family and friends and improve your child's behavior. Managing stress, improving your emotional well-being, and helping your child thrive is easier when you build a supportive network and prioritize your needs. Each small step counts towards progress when parenting a child with ODD.

Lend Your Voice to ODD Parenting Support

Dear Reader,

I sincerely hope that this book has provided valuable insights and guidance on your journey to better understand and support your child with Oppositional Defiant Disorder.

Your experience as a parent of a child with ODD is unique, and sharing your honest thoughts about this book can make a significant difference for other parents who are seeking reliable resources. By leaving a genuine review on Amazon, you'll help guide them towards a source of support and encouragement in their parenting journey.

As an independent author, your feedback directly impacts the visibility and reach of my book. If you could take a few moments to write an honest review on Amazon, I would be incredibly grateful. I will personally read each review and take your insights to heart.

Scan to leave a review

Your opinions, whether positive or negative, are truly valuable to me and to others seeking guidance in the world of ODD parenting. Thank you for taking the time to share your thoughts, and I look forward to reading your review.

Warm regards,

Erika.

Conclusion

In the case of raising a child who has been diagnosed with oppositional defiant disorder (ODD), any parent can face considerable difficulties. Dealing with a persistently defiant and resistant child can be incredibly frustrating and exhausting. Due to the tendency of those children to argue and resist authority and test limits, children with ODD can be a source of stress and difficulty for their parents.

Unfortunately, parents of children with ODD often feel alone and unsupported in their struggles with raising children with ODD. If you are going through a tough moment, know you are not alone, and that resources are available to assist you in coping with it.

Reaching out to friends, family, or a professional for support can help alleviate some of the stress and frustration associated with parenting a child with ODD. Getting to know other parents going through similar struggles as you are through a support group for parents of children with ODD may be helpful.

I wrote this book to supply you with all the basics you need to deal with children suffering from ODD. When facing a child with ODD, it is not easy to know how to deal with them, but it is important to remember that every family dynamic is different. When raising an oppositional defiant disorder child, it is extremely important to choose the appropriate technique to use. As important as it is to know the basic concepts of parenting a child with ODD, it is also essential that you tailor your approach to your child's specific needs to be successful.

It is important to first learn as much as possible about ODD, including its signs and symptoms and how it is diagnosed and treated. As a result of this information, you can better understand and control your child's behavior. As a next step, you should be able to establish firm limits and guidelines for your child so that they will know what is expected of them and the consequences of disobeying you. There should be a consistent application of consequences, and power battles should be avoided as much as possible. As a parent, it is essential that you remain calm when dealing with a child who has oppositional defiant disorder so that they do not get out of hand. Whenever possible, encourage good habits with rewards and compliments, and if you need help or advice, reach out to family members and professionals. Participating in a support group for parents of children with a behavior disorder may also be beneficial for you as a parent.

The most important thing you should do is find a strategy that helps you and your kids. Since there are no universally applicable guidelines for handling an ODD child, parents must consider their unique situation while developing a parenting strategy.

Make sure you take your time, do not give up, and do not be afraid to ask for assistance if you need it. Parenting is difficult no matter the circumstances, including parenting a kid with oppositional defiant disorder, but it is bigger than any hurdle.

About the Author

Erika Bishop is a dedicated parent, mentor, and advocate for children and families facing the challenges of behavioral disorders. With a compassionate heart and a wealth of personal experience, Erika offers guidance and support to parents navigating the often tumultuous journey of raising a child with complex behavioral needs.

Erika's passion for helping families stemmed from her own experiences in raising a child diagnosed with a behavioral disorder. Recognizing the lack of resources and support available, she embarked on a mission to educate herself on evidence-based techniques and strategies to better understand and manage the complexities of various disorders. Over the years, Erika has gained invaluable insights and developed effective tools for fostering a healthy and nurturing environment for children with diverse needs.

Erika's commitment to making a difference in the lives of children and families led her to create a support network for parents dealing with similar challenges. Through this community, she has empowered countless families to find the strength, patience, and understanding needed to transform their parenting experience.

In her writing, Erika shares her knowledge and expertise, offering readers practical advice, strategies, and techniques to foster a loving and supportive home environment for children with behavioral challenges. Her empathetic approach to parenting encourages open communication, mutual respect, and unconditional love, helping families overcome the unique obstacles they face.

When Erika is not writing or mentoring, she is an avid reader and enjoys exploring the outdoors with her family. She believes in the transformative power of mindfulness and incorporates meditation and yoga into her daily routine. Erika is passionate about helping others find hope and healing, and her dedication to making a positive impact in the lives of children and families has made her a respected figure in the field of parenting and behavioral disorders.

Printed in Great Britain
by Amazon